The Teal Revolution

The
Crikey.
Read

The Teal Revolution

Inside the movement changing Australian politics

MARGOT SAVILLE

Hardie Grant

BOOKS

Published in 2022 by Hardie Grant Books,
an imprint of Hardie Grant Publishing

Hardie Grant Books (Melbourne)
Wurundjeri Country
Building 1, 658 Church Street
Richmond, Victoria 3121

Hardie Grant Books (London)
5th & 6th Floors
52–54 Southwark Street
London SE1 1UN

hardiegrant.com/au/books

A catalogue record for this
book is available from the
National Library of Australia

The Teal Revolution
ISBN 978 1 74379 930 7

10 9 8 7 6 5 4 3 2 1

Cover design by Design by Committee
Typeset in Adobe Caslon Pro by Cannon Typesetting

Printed in Australia by Griffin Press, an Accredited
ISO AS/NZS 14001 Environmental Management System printer.

The paper this book is printed on is certified against the
Forest Stewardship Council® Standards. Griffin Press holds
chain of custody certification SGSHK-COC-005088.
FSC® promotes environmentally responsible, socially
beneficial and economically viable management of the
world's forests.

Hardie Grant acknowledges the Traditional Owners of the country on which we
work, the Wurundjeri people of the Kulin nation and the Gadigal people of the
Eora nation, and recognises their continuing connection to the land, waters and
culture. We pay our respects to their Elders past and present.

CONTENTS

PROLOGUE

ELECTION NIGHT

Saturday, 21 May 2022 in Melbourne and Sydney was horrendous. Torrential rain and freezing winds swept both cities; jumpers, rain jackets and umbrellas were essential as people lined up to vote.

Two women in these cities had not met, but they had much in common. They were running as community independents in largely similar electorates – Dr Monique Ryan in the inner-eastern Melbourne electorate of Kooyong and Allegra Spender in Wentworth in Sydney's Eastern Suburbs. The voters of both electorates were well educated and wealthy; they cared about climate change, political integrity and equality for women.

As the winds dropped and the day darkened, both women, who had been standing and talking to voters for almost ten hours in their respective seats, started to pack up. There was nothing more they could do.

At about 5.30 pm, Monique Ryan drove home from the polling booth with campaign chair Ann Capling, crying. Both women were devastated; they thought they'd lost. But Ryan knew she'd run the best possible campaign. 'And I thought it was just a bit unfair that I had the tough one,' she told me later. Kooyong's sitting member was treasurer Josh Frydenberg. 'I thought if I had Tim Wilson or Jason Falinski, I could have taken them down, but Josh was just a bridge too far.'

Ryan went home and tried to focus on her speech. 'But I couldn't write it because I was too upset. I just couldn't … and so I had a good old howl.'

At this point her husband, Peter Jordan, came home and gave her the sort of 'pull yourself together' pep talk that spouses excel at. He told her there were 1200 people at the Auburn Hotel in Hawthorn waiting for her to arrive and she had to turn up and thank them. The paediatric neurologist took a deep breath, had a shower and got ready to go out.

As they arrived at the pub around 7 pm, the scrutineers were phoning in the first results and told her it was 50/50 on first preferences. Ryan dismissed this news as some sort of statistical anomaly.

Later in the evening she did a live cross to the Nine Network's election coverage, where former deputy Liberal leader Julie Bishop told her she would probably win the seat. Ryan refused to believe it, telling supporters she would wait until more votes had been counted.

Finally, at about 9.30 pm, the ABC's election expert Antony Green said Frydenberg was not going to get above 43 per cent of the vote. At this point, everyone in the Auburn Hotel started screaming their lungs out. It was pandemonium.

The Age took a photo after that moment of Ryan embracing her brother Peter, her eyes closed and head resting on his shoulder. They were having a quiet moment to remember Peter's son Hector, who had died in a car crash at the age of eighteen.

The long-time Kooyong resident said she was so stressed during the night that she had chest pains, plus a sore head from the deafening noise levels. 'No one anticipated it was going to turn out as well as it did; we thought that might be a hung parliament, and hopefully there'd be three independents with the balance of power. You know, we didn't think it was going to be a change of government and almost all the indies would get in … I couldn't quite believe it.'

It's an Australian tradition that an incoming politician can't claim victory until the loser has conceded. So Ryan waited for days for Frydenberg to concede. Finally, he rang. As Ryan tells it, the now-former treasurer was struggling with what to say.

'He basically said, "My team thinks I should call you and obviously the numbers aren't good." And then he just stopped, and I said, "Well, obviously it's a tough call for you to make, Josh, and thank you. Thank you for your twelve years of service and many people feel that you've done a great job as a local member." … And then he said, "Well, I'm glad you said that because I felt that your campaign was not really run in the right spirit."'

The defeated member for Kooyong never uttered the words 'you won' or 'congratulations'. Frydenberg, a former tennis champ, was offering no polite handshake over the net.

* * *

In Wentworth, as the polls closed, an exhausted Allegra Spender met her family at her sister Bianca's house where their brother and his family were waiting. The three siblings and their nine children sat down for a pizza dinner. Phones were banned.

The forty-four-year-old had visited around ten election booths that day, accompanied by campaign director Lyndell Droga and Lyndell's husband Daniel, who'd come along as driver. Spender was wearing her favourite jacket, a pale-blue blazer that had been designed and owned by her late mother, Carla Zampatti. Every time Spender put it on, she looked at the tiny pin hole in the lapel where Carla had placed her Order of Australia pin; wearing it gave her confidence.

At one of the booths, a seven-year-old girl had asked her if she was nervous. 'And I said, "I am. I'm nervous and I'm not nervous because on the one hand I've done everything I can now and so if I lose, I lose. I can't say I've left anything on the table and now it's not in my control."'

At about 7.30 pm she went to the Drogas' house where the campaign team was gathered, reading early results off laptops. An hour later, the signs were looking good, although Spender thought the seat would still be in play.

With husband Mark Capps and the Drogas, she made her way to the Bondi Bowling Club, where her team's party was underway. About 600 people, mostly wearing campaign T-shirts, were clustered around a few televisions, eating spring rolls and having a few well-earned drinks.

The former chief executive knew she would have to have three forms of words ready: for victory, defeat or uncertainty. 'The speeches were very similar. Because the whole point of this was about the community, and regardless of what the actual outcome was, we knew we've made enough noise in the community. We had already made a difference.'

As she entered the party around 9 pm, the in-house DJ queued up the opening bars of The Black Eyed Peas' 'I Gotta Feeling'; the TV cameras captured Allegra and Bianca dancing and laughing together, enjoying the moment. By the time

Aretha Franklin's 'Respect' and Pharrell Williams' 'Happy' came on the playlist, the entire crowd was dancing and singing. Spender made a very slow progress through the crowd, trying to shake as many hands and thank as many people as possible.

Lyndell Droga took to the stage at about 10.30 pm and acknowledged the independent women who had blazed a trail, including Cathy McGowan, Zali Steggall and former Wentworth independent MP Kerryn Phelps.

Spender then came on to say that it had been 'a victory for the community movement around the country. We stand for the future, not for the past. You've given up shouting at the television, the negativity and the spin. You've all invested in the democracy of the country'.[1]

Spender and Capps left the party at midnight and made their way home, just in time to hear Antony Green call the seat in her favour.

With three young children, there was no sleep-in the next morning; instead she let them colour in the picture of 'Mummy' on a corflute before she headed out to a media conference on Bondi Beach. Later that afternoon, Dave Sharma called to graciously concede defeat and congratulate her on her victory.

Monique Ryan made her way home via Campaign HQ, where there was a deafening dance party in progress. The next morning, she was back outside the office at 6.30 am doing a TV interview. When the journalist suggested they go inside, she politely refused. 'God knows what's behind those doors.'

1.

WHO ARE THE TEALS?

At the 2022 federal election, the Coalition government suffered a major defeat, losing eighteen seats and the election to Anthony Albanese's Australian Labor Party. But the big story wasn't the winning strategy of Labor. All anyone wanted to talk about were the six independent female candidates who had achieved the almost impossible: displacing their high-profile Liberal Party opponents, including the treasurer, in what had been blue-blood Liberal electorates. The media had christened them the 'Teals', a name that reflects both the colour most used in their campaigns and their ideological position – a mix of blue, for conservative liberal economic values, and green, for their focus on effective action on climate change.

These six women had received money from Simon Holmes à Court's group, Climate 200, which donated $13 million to twenty-three candidates in total, including David Pocock, who won his Senate race. Climate 200 also gave funds to the independent campaigns of Zali Steggall, Helen Haines, Rebekha Sharkie and Andrew Wilkie, who were already MPs.

But when the word 'Teal' was used in the media, it was almost always used to describe this group of six accomplished women.

Although these women have a lot in common, they strenuously resist the group label and prefer to be dealt with as individuals. Their most obvious similarity – they're all women – can be expanded to describe them all as middle-class white women who live in and now represent very affluent communities. Clearly, their success is not a complete victory for diversity, but politics is the 'art of the possible', not the desirable. Cultural change can be slow.

How did they do it? The six campaigns were very different, but there were common elements. All were run in wealthy metropolitan seats with highly educated voters and 'moderate' incumbent Liberal MPs. The Teals' messaging channelled community anger about the inability of these men (and they were mostly men) to influence their party on climate action, political integrity and gender equality. The campaigns had outstanding professional candidates, each backed by a formidable team, thousands of volunteers and substantial amounts of money.

Finally, they had something both parties lacked: a desire to put policy-making ahead of politicking.

As the chair of the Wentworth campaign, Lyndell Droga, said about their candidate: 'Part of the winning formula of Allegra is that she doesn't need anything. She doesn't need fame, so she wasn't doing it for that reason. She doesn't need power, she doesn't need money. She's purely driven by policy, not by politics.' You could say this about every one of the Teals.

These six women had grasped the concept that the world is run by the people who show up – and they showed up. Their campaigns included more than 10,000 volunteers who knocked on over 100,000 doors, made 50,000-odd phone calls and generated 100,000 media mentions. It was a revolution.

Anthropologist Margaret Mead once wrote: 'Never doubt that a small group of thoughtful, committed citizens can change the world. Indeed, it is the only thing that ever has.' She was proved right. A total of 200,071 Australian electors decided they wanted change and voted for the six Teals. Their model disrupted a political system built on a ruthless duopoly and high barriers to entry.

* * *

Every one of the Teals – in Sydney, Allegra Spender in Wentworth, Kylea Tink in North Sydney and Dr Sophie Scamps in Mackellar; in Melbourne, Dr Monique Ryan in Kooyong and Zoe Daniel in Goldstein; and Kate Chaney in Perth's Curtin – is like many of the women in their electorates. They're highly educated professional women juggling stellar careers with very busy family lives.

Spender has an economics degree from Cambridge University and a master's from the University of London and was the CEO of the Australian Business and Community Network. Tink has a communications degree and was the CEO of the McGrath Foundation. Scamps has a master's degree from Oxford University (and an athletics blue) and ran a busy medical practice. Ryan was the director of the neurology department at the Royal Children's Hospital in Melbourne. Daniel has a journalism degree, is the author of three well-reviewed books and worked as an ABC foreign correspondent for twenty-seven years. Chaney has a law degree and an MBA and was a senior executive with Anglicare WA.

All have taken their professional qualifications and used them to help society, rather than just enrich themselves. And unlike many female politicians of the past, all have children.

To give context, very few women – particularly women with children, and without a political party to back them – can afford to work unpaid on a project for six to nine months with no guaranteed job to go back to if it fails. You need to have savings to fall back on as well as a supportive partner. Most of the candidates paid credit to their husbands, who by default became sole breadwinners while their partners campaigned. In addition, they all live in communities with the capacity to donate substantial amounts of money and time; volunteering presupposes that you're not worried about paying the rent.

However, there is one glaring gap in the Teals' illustrious résumés. None has taken the conventional path to winning office by joining a political party at a young age, crawling through the trenches of Young Liberals or Young Labor and then going to work for an MP. None has had the time, appetite or inclination to spend hours plotting to overthrow factional archenemies or stacking branches to smooth their path to pre-selection. They've had real lives.

That's not to say that they haven't been connected to politics. Ryan and Chaney have both been members of the ALP. Spender and Chaney come from Liberal Party dynasties – Allegra's father John Spender and grandfather Sir Percy Spender were Liberal politicians. Kate's uncle Fred Chaney was a Liberal politician for almost twenty years, and his father Sir Frederick Chaney was a minister in the government of Sir Robert Menzies.

Since the election, many Liberal politicians have come out to say that these women should have been pre-selected as Liberal candidates, but it's fanciful to think they would have been. First, thanks to weapons-grade factional in-fighting and the absence of a female quota in the Liberal Party, they would not have made it past the first stage, knocked out by some private schoolboy with a Hugh Grant haircut and no chin. More importantly, none would have considered associating with a political brand that is widely viewed as toxic to women.

If anyone had any doubts about the Liberal Party's ingrained misogyny, those were dispelled when the eighty-two-year-old former prime minister John Howard described the Teals as 'groupies'. 'I've had enough of this crap,' thought many women. 'I'm going to vote these dinosaurs out.'

All six Teals had a conviction that politics was broken, as shown by the lack of action on climate change. Years of efforts to get action to avert a climate crisis – the marching, the petitions, the lobbying, the campaigning – had been stymied by a loose confederation of climate sceptics, fossil fuel companies and conservative politicians. As detailed in Marian Wilkinson's book *The Carbon Club*, this group successfully lobbied politicians and manipulated public opinion, resulting in successive governments failing to take decisive action on climate change.[2]

After years of frustration, these women worked out that the current two-party system wasn't going to deliver; the only way to solve the impasse was to elect an independent who could break the gridlock and demand action.

But the Teals did not spring up election-ready; they had two main outside sources of help. The first was the community organisations behind them, often over a thousand people per candidate, which developed from the grassroots.

This was overlaid with the money and expertise of Climate 200. According to Monique Ryan, 'without the support of Climate 200 it would have been very difficult for us to have the audacity to take on the treasurer of Australia in the bluest of blue-ribbon seats'.

Although hostile media described the Teal independents as 'Climate 200–backed candidates' during the campaign, the money from Holmes à Court's organisation made up only part of their coffers – between a third and a half of the total. All six campaigns raised many hundreds of thousands of dollars, not all of it from people in their electorates.

These funds enabled the campaigns to mount groundbreaking digital advertising campaigns and hire world-class strategists. The social capital in the community organisations, combined with the financial and intellectual capital of Climate 200 and donations, proved to be unbeatable in those six seats. The Liberal Party, which was still mounting topdown analogue election campaigns, was blindsided by the digital natives.

A short history of change at kitchen tables

The tectonic plates that led to the seismic shift of 2022 really started moving ten years earlier, when a business consultant in rural north-east Victoria called Cathy McGowan looked around her community and thought, 'Something has to change.'

McGowan's niece and nephew – who, like most young people in the area, had been forced to move to Melbourne to find meaningful work – were the first to suggest to McGowan the idea to make the Liberal stronghold of Indi marginal and for her to run as an independent candidate.

McGowan writes in her book *Cathy Goes to Canberra* that her niece and nephew considered the situation in the villages and towns of Indi as hopeless.[3] 'They told me, "The trains didn't work, there was little if any mobile phone coverage, no internet, few jobs and no-one cared about climate change."' Decades of loyal voting for LNP candidates making it a safe seat had not produced much of a return, 'and they reckoned this shouldn't be allowed to go on'.

The young relatives had caught McGowan in a reflective mood. A month earlier, her father had died. She was fifty-eight years old, she wrote, and thought that this was the right time to get on with her life. If she was going to be effecting positive changes in the world around her, she'd have to start 'creating the change [she] wanted to see'.

McGowan eventually agreed to take part in a campaign, although she insisted that her main role was to find the right candidate. In 2013, she and her colleagues formed Voices for Indi and started a process they called Kitchen Table Conversations.[4] Hosts would invite family and friends to an informal venue, often literally a kitchen table, for a one-hour meeting with refreshments. There, attendees would be asked to answer a handful of questions: 'What do you love about north-east Victoria? What do you want out of a representative? What are your issues?' Each host was provided with a kit that explained the process and expectations, as well as questionnaires to fill out.

Four months later, in May 2013, Voices for Indi collated the responses to those conversations and released a sixteen-page report.

'We wanted to make sure everybody could find their words there and we didn't try to come up with a little, hard summary or give any larger meaning to it,' McGowan recalled in her book. 'We were saying, "Here's what we've heard." … It was a way of showing voters that we already had a strong community; all we had to do was recognise that and harness ourselves to it in the four months between then and election day.'

During this process, McGowan grew more comfortable with the idea of running as a candidate. 'A lot of people had been telling me they wanted me to do it, so in the end I was happy to say yes. After all, I thought it wasn't as if we were going to win; it would just be a finite and relatively brief period of campaigning and then I could go back to my work.'

She ran as the independent candidate for Indi in the federal election of September 2013. Although the Coalition won the election and Tony Abbott became prime minister, McGowan won the seat, ending the career of right-wing factional warrior Sophie Mirabella.

At the next election, in 2016, despite the Liberal Party throwing everything it could at their Indi campaign, McGowan won again, increasing her margin by 5 per cent. By 2019, she was keen to retire and Voices for Indi candidate Helen Haines won the seat, becoming the first independent in Australian history to succeed another independent in a federal seat.

In Indi, the issues were similar to those in the Teal seats, but the demographics were different; the residents of rural seats tend to be older and poorer than their urban counterparts, with lower levels of education. But when Haines went to Canberra in 2019, she sat on the crossbench with a woman whose constituency did look more like a Teal electorate: Zali Steggall, the member for Warringah.

Even before she entered parliament, Steggall was famous. The forty-eight-year-old won medals at the Winter Olympics and the World Championships, making her this country's most successful alpine skier on the world stage. Her grandfather Jack Steggall played ten Tests for Australia in rugby union and her brother is Olympic snowboarder Zeke Steggall; this is a family that is used to competing – and winning. After retiring from skiing, she completed an arts/law degree and became a barrister.

Steggall's campaign in Warringah began in 2018 when a group of residents in Manly and Mosman, two of Sydney's most affluent suburbs, decided that local MP and former PM

Tony Abbott was blocking progress on climate change. Inspired by McGowan and Voices for Indi, these residents started up their own community group, Voices of Warringah, and began a series of Kitchen Table Conversations. They were supported by two existing organisations, Vote Tony Out and Time's Up Tony, both of which produced merchandise sold around the country. Steggall won the seat convincingly, despatching one of the country's most polarising political figures back to the bike shed.

I met Steggall before the 2019 election; in person she is charming and funny, with a good line in self-deprecation. But I sensed the steel beneath the surface, which is hardly surprising in a former world-class athlete. When first observing the Teals, I compared them unfavourably to the former Olympic skier, thinking they lacked her competitiveness and fighting spirit; happily, they've proved me wrong.

McGowan is called the 'Godmother of the Teals' for being the inspiration for their campaigns. All have acknowledged that the revolution that sent six women to Canberra in 2022 had begun a decade earlier in an Indigo Valley farmhouse. But somewhere along the way it was turbocharged by alternative energy investor Simon Holmes à Court.

The fifty-year-old businessman is the son of Australia's first billionaire, the late Robert Holmes à Court, and philanthropist Janet Holmes à Court. He was brought up to believe that he could and should challenge the status quo – his father was famously iconoclastic – and leave the world a better place.

In 2019, Holmes à Court was on the board of the Australian Environmental Grantmakers Network, a group that helped philanthropists donate with more impact. He later told the *7am* podcast that no matter what they did, the Grantmakers Network's great ideas hit a brick wall in Canberra.[5]

'We were hacking at the branches when striking at the root meant we needed to have a majority of MPs that wanted a science-based response to climate change [and were committed to restoring] integrity to politics,' he said. 'So Climate 200's job was to work towards having a majority of MPs that support climate and integrity.'

Inspired by McGowan's campaign, he formed Climate 200 and crowdfunded money to give to climate-focused independent candidates in the 2019 election. In just ten weeks, a group of people, including tech billionaire Mike Cannon-Brookes, donated a total of $500,000. This was distributed to a few candidates, including Haines and Rebekha Sharkie, who retained her South Australian seat of Mayo. Although Oliver Yates in Kooyong and Kerryn Phelps in Wentworth didn't win, they did manage to turn the seats into marginal ones. The businessman had had his first taste of climate-based political activism and was hooked.

* * *

I started covering Allegra Spender's campaign in November 2021 and went to most of her public events, particularly during the campaign. I also attended events with Kylea Tink and another independent candidate, Nicolette Boele. Early on, *Crikey* editor Peter Fray mentioned that there might be a book in the Teals, so I started taking notes, little knowing at the time that six would win their seats. If only I'd looked at Sportsbet and placed my *Crikey* income on them succeeding, I'd have written this book in St Barts.

Since the election, the Wentworth Independents – the small group backing Spender's successful campaign – have very generously opened up their diaries and contact books to help me understand what happened, as have countless people on all the other campaigns. Unlike every other political story I've written, it's been a universally positive experience, with almost no evidence of bad faith or foul play. The Teals really are a new breed of politician.

A final word on one crucial element of this story. The signature colour that has given these politicians their nickname is in fact a misnomer.

When the community independents started their campaigns, choosing a colour was one of the hardest decisions they faced. Colours are a vital part of any branding – when you spy a sea of people in red T-shirts around a polling booth, you automatically know they are Labor. But most colours are taken: the Coalition is royal blue, the Greens are green, One Nation is orange and Clive Palmer's UAP is bright yellow. Kylea Tink uses a retina-searing salmon colour called 'Tink pink', the Australian Electoral Commission uses purple, and black shirts have an unfortunate historical connotation.

Zali Steggall once told *The Sydney Morning Herald* that she had chosen 'blue with a touch of green' as her colour because it made sense to represent the Warringah area and its beaches, and it spoke to what she stood for as being 'fiscally responsible but strong on environment'.[6]

The Olympic champion was happy for the new wave of blue-green candidates to adopt her colour and her methods. 'It's a bit like a franchise,' she told *The Age*. 'You replicate a model that works, but you do it independently. The people who attack us and say we're a party are missing the point.'[7]

But for the love of the Pantone colour chart, please – it's not teal, it's turquoise.

2.

TURNING TIDES: NEW SOUTH WALES

The mood for change in the Teal electorates was ignited by the bushfires of 2019–2020, which made real the consequences of climate change. Just a few months later, COVID-19 spread to Australia and most of the urban areas went into lockdown.

With the federal government floundering, it was up to the state governments to manage the COVID response. In the country's two biggest states, Victorian Labor premier Dan Andrews and NSW Coalition premier Gladys Berejiklian became the faces of the pandemic, each fronting up for a daily press conference.

Andrews imposed the world's longest lockdown, becoming a polarising leader who was loved and loathed in equal measure. Berejiklian adopted a more managerial style and fewer lockdowns, maintaining her existing popularity.

In Western Australia, Labor premier Mark McGowan sealed off the state from the rest of the country for around 700 days, trying to achieve COVID Zero. The locals approved, delivering him an historic landslide victory at the March 2021 state election, where Labor won fifty-three out of fifty-nine lower house seats.

In general, differences between the Teal candidates reflect this state-based history. The three NSW Teals sound a little more conservative and the Victorian and WA Teals a little more progressive. After climate change, Spender and Scamps campaigned strongly on economic issues like tax reform and fiscal repair, while in August Zoe Daniel announced she would instigate a motion for a judicial inquiry into media concentration, a traditionally progressive issue. When it came time to writing these chapters, it became clear that this was the best way to split them up – separating the bluer seats in NSW from the remaining seats in Victoria and WA.

To set our scene in NSW, Wentworth and North Sydney are both inner-urban seats, while Mackellar is much further out, on the Northern Beaches of Sydney. The southernmost suburb of Mackellar, North Curl Curl, is about 17 kilometres from the city, about an hour in peak-hour traffic. Early polling showed that climate change was the number one priority for the urban seats, while the issue sat lower down in Mackellar, below the economy and cost of living. But over the course of the campaign, it matched the others by creeping up to first place.

All three incumbent MPs were 'moderate' Liberals. When they saw polls starting to favour the Teal candidates, they tried a form of emotional blackmail on their voters: 'Get rid of me and you'll get Peter Dutton.' It didn't work.

Sydney takes shape

The second week of February 2021 was searingly hot – on some days, temperatures were ten degrees above the average. With the inner city humid and unbearable, Woollahra couple

Maria Atkinson and Michael Joseph decamped to the northern Sydney suburb of Palm Beach to stay with friends.

Sunday was Atkinson's birthday; after rising they went for a long walk and flung themselves into the pounding surf. On the way back they dropped in for breakfast with another visiting Woollahra couple, Lyndell and Daniel Droga. As the men tucked into eggs and bacon on the deck, the two women went inside the house.

Atkinson was in a contemplative mood – birthdays were a reminder that time was passing. She told Lyndell that she'd formed a group to find an independent candidate to stand in their electorate of Wentworth in the Eastern Suburbs – someone like Zali Steggall in Warringah.

'Do you want to be involved?'

Lyndell thought for a second and replied, 'I'm in.'

Weeks later, Lyndell and Maria formed Wentworth Independents, then found Allegra Spender – and the rest is history.

But the seed of this idea had in fact been planted a few years earlier when Atkinson, an environmental consultant, was on the Greater Sydney Commission with architect Rod Simpson. After meetings, they had coffee and shared their frustration over government inaction on climate change. Simpson told Atkinson about the 'Voices' groups that had been springing up around the country: non-partisan community groups, including Voices for Indi, channelling frustration with the two-party political system. Atkinson was interested but, with a busy career, had no time to start a Voices of Wentworth group.

Life went on, but her frustration with the lack of action on climate change continued to build. The tipping point was the Black Summer of 2019–20, when bushfires raged up and down the east coast of Australia.

In early December, as Atkinson travelled into the Sydney CBD to attend the National Smart Energy Summit, acrid smoke blanketed the city. Air filters and face masks sold out as doctors warned asthmatics and people with lung disease to stay indoors; air quality was eleven times worse than hazardous levels.

It was starting to get political. At the conference, NSW environment minister Matt Kean contradicted his federal Coalition counterparts, saying that climate change lay behind the bushfire crisis and that emissions reduction was essential. He told the delegates that weather conditions were 'exactly what the scientists have warned us would happen. Longer drier periods, resulting in more drought and bushfires. If this is not a catalyst for change, then I don't know what is'.[8]

Former PM Malcolm Turnbull, who had been deposed by the right-wing forces in his party just a year beforehand, also addressed the conference. He said that the debate over climate change was stuck, with many refusing to acknowledge the science and instead stubbornly – and blindly – holding to their political positions.

'As we head into 2020 we don't have an emissions trading scheme ... because of the inability to get the National Energy Guarantee through the Coalition party room [due to] a minority of destructive climate change deniers,' he told the summit. 'Now, the tragedy is that climate change has become a political battlefield and an issue of belief and religion, whereas in fact, it should just be about physics and science.'[9]

Atkinson went home feeling determined; if the government wasn't going to listen to the science, it was time to change the government.

She wasn't the only one to have been spurred into action by the bushfires. In the Northern Beaches of Sydney, Dr Sophie Scamps was standing at her front gate, anxiously looking at the smoke filling the sky. From her letterbox, she took a flyer from local Liberal MP Jason Falinski listing the electorate's most important issues. She looked in vain for the words 'climate change'.

There was, however, an invitation to a 'Meet the MP Meet-Up' and Scamps went along.

'At that time we'd been hearing non-stop from Craig Kelly, Matt Canavan and Barnaby Joyce that arsonists were starting fires rather than climate change,' she told the Croakey website. 'We said to the MP, "We need to hear your voice if you're a moderate." He replied: "The problem is, you can't mention the words climate change in the party room because the Queensland MPs jump up and down."'[10]

Scamps thought, 'How are you representing us?' That's when she realised that the electors of the very safe Liberal seat of Mackellar were being ignored and taken for granted.

In January, reports came from China about a deadly new virus named COVID-19. Every day, there were stories about its lethal virulence and geographic spread. In March, most of the urban areas of Australia went into lockdown. Many people found themselves at home, perhaps with more time and energy to connect with their local community groups via Zoom and talk about things that mattered to them, including taking action on climate change.

Scamps spoke to her twelve-year-old son and his friends about climate change in this time, telling them it would be an issue for them. 'Yes, because you adults have failed us,' one replied.

She related this story in her first speech to parliament. 'His comment found its target. I listened and I decided to act. As Cathy McGowan puts it so frequently, I realised that there was no cavalry coming over the hill to save us; there was only us. I had to do whatever I could to make a difference. If not you, then who?'

Scamps and her colleagues in the local environmental group realised that the main problem was at federal level. 'We thought we could bring about change, but it became pretty clear that wasn't going to happen because within the party system, our representative was very hamstrung and had to toe the party line,' she later reflected.

At a local meeting about solar power, she met a woman who had worked on Steggall's campaign, who told her about the Voices movement. Scamps went home and made a few notes.

During lockdown, many other people were considering emulating Voices for Indi and creating their own community group. In April, Rod Simpson, his partner Andrea Wilson and art director Felicity Coonan started Voices of North Sydney. They held well over a hundred Kitchen Table Conversations to find out the issues that mattered to the community.

Wilson said that they then met with Liberal MP Trent Zimmerman to discuss their findings. 'At that meeting, it became very clear that there would be no deviation from the party line.'

North Sydney has the important legacy of Ted Mack, who was the independent member from 1990 to 1996 after a very successful career in local and state government.

'He worked hard to put in place mechanisms that involve people in the decision-making process. This took various forms, but the precinct committee structure that he put in place when he was in local government continues to this day, almost fifty years later.' This was a significant point of difference for North Sydney that could be built on, Wilson said.[11]

In May, Voices of North Sydney held their first Zoom town hall meeting to discuss the topic 'Are we being represented?

How democratic are we and is there a gap between the issues of concern and how our federal representative has voted?' Looking up 'moderate' Liberal MP Trent Zimmerman's voting record, they were underwhelmed.[12]

Over on the other side of Sydney Harbour, in the suburb of Randwick in the Eastern Suburbs, lawyer Kath Naish was frustrated. She had watched the 2019 election result with despair, fearing that action on climate change was now out of contention. With two children in primary school, she was worried that their future was being compromised.

'There was this idea that was starting to emerge [that] we need to maybe start a Voices group in Wentworth that can start to engage with the community,' she told me. The idea was to put pressure on the local member, Dave Sharma, and get him to listen to the community. 'So it wasn't really originally about putting an independent in,' she recalled, 'but more about just getting the community engaged around climate action, which was the key issue, and approaching him and getting him to act'.

For Naish there was another motivation; a few years earlier, she had been successfully treated for breast cancer. 'It really made me look very hard at myself and about what I wanted to do with my time and my energy ... So the penny really dropped for me after the 2019 election when I realised that no one was coming to sort this problem out. It was going to come down to people like me and other people that I knew to really do something.'

Frustrated at Sharma's unresponsiveness to questions about climate, Naish realised that one voter wasn't going to get anywhere; it needed to be a collective voice. With friends Eliana Leopold and Delia Burrage, she set up the Voices of Wentworth website and social media presence.

One of the key debates inside all these community organisations was whether to stay positive – gathering views and having a dialogue with the local member – or turn into an activist organisation that tries to vote the sitting member out. While the founding members of Voices of North Sydney decided to stay positive, another local resident, media executive Denise Shrivell, chose to turn activist and started Time's Up Trent. It was loosely based on the Warringah group, Time's Up Tony, and highlighted the disconnect between Zimmerman's public statements and his voting record.

In June, Voices of North Sydney held their second Zoom town hall with Voices for Indi's Alana Johnson, a cattle farmer and pioneer of rural women's leadership, as guest speaker. She told the listeners that an independent candidate could maximise effectiveness by concentrating on a few issues rather than attempting a broad policy platform. Cooped up inside due to a miserable winter, looking for a distraction from the news of the pandemic and seeking a figurative window to the outside world, people were jumping online to watch and engage.

Around the same time, Scamps, her friend Anyo Geddes and three other like-minded women created Voices of Mackellar. They conducted Kitchen Table Conversations with almost 500 members of the voting public, asking about what they valued in their communities, what issues concerned them most and what they looked for in their political representatives.

Voices of Wentworth held their first town hall meeting in July, also on Zoom. Wentworth resident and environmental activist Blair Palese, who co-founded environmental group 350.org in 2009, spoke about the need to get the federal government to act on climate change.

A few months later, the group organised a second virtual town hall meeting, this time on the topic of economic recovery and climate change. Maria Atkinson spoke, along with Monica Richter, an economist and social ecologist with experience in sustainability; both women had been introduced to Naish by Palese. Critical networks were starting to form.

Naish said that they asked Sharma several times to come to the town hall events and to be on the panels. After each event they would write to him with summaries and ask him to take action on various initiatives, including Helen Haines' integrity bill (to establish a federal integrity commission) and Zali Steggall's emissions reduction bill.

Sharma sent them a few non-committal responses. 'It became pretty clear that he wasn't going to change his vote. He was going to carry on toeing the line and doing what Scott Morrison told him,' Naish said.

Momentum builds

The Smart Energy Council is Australia's independent body for renewable energy. At its annual conference in September 2020, Morrison and the minister for energy and emissions reduction, Angus Taylor, spoke about a gas-led recovery. Maria Atkinson attended and listened, incredulous. She thought, 'You're kidding me, when we've had bushfires? That's our future?'

At the same conference, Malcolm Turnbull told attendees that the only workaround to the issue was electing independents. 'So that's when lots of people texted me and said, "Enough. Something needs to be done,"' Atkinson said.

Just a few weeks later, on 13 October, a formidable group gathered around Lucy Turnbull's kitchen table. Over finger food and tea, Atkinson, Palese, Richter and Turnbull talked about how to take action on climate change. Turnbull had also invited along someone who was unknown to the others: climate investor Kirsty Gold, from the Warringah campaign.

Gold, one of the most important figures in the community independent movement, laid out for the group all the details of the plan to get rid of Abbott, a climate change sceptic. As an aside, has Tony Abbott ever reflected on the important part he played in the rise of the community independents movement? Just by being so polarising, he galvanised some very impressive women to start a revolution.

A trained accountant and former partner at PwC, Gold sits on the board of the Climate Council and runs a climate fund called Assembly Climate Capital. Determined to defeat Abbott, she had co-founded the group Warringah Independent and helped to build the campaign from the ground up. She has offered advice to many other community independent groups, including those in the NSW electorates of North Sydney, Mackellar, Hughes and Hume, as well as Wentworth.

At one point, Malcolm Turnbull wandered into the kitchen to get a cup of tea, asking, 'What are you lot cooking up?' They didn't enlighten him.

After Gold left, the group talked about whether such a plan could succeed in Wentworth. For Atkinson, this was a 'lightning bolt moment' – she could foresee how the plan she'd had milling around in her head might actually work.

Three days later, Atkinson and Gold met again to talk through the specifics of how to run an effective campaign; the consultant took copious notes.

There were now two groups in Wentworth using different methods to achieve the same aim: getting action on climate change. Atkinson and her colleagues were attempting to replace Sharma with an independent, while Voices of Wentworth had decided to remain a non-partisan community group.

Voices of Wentworth founder Kath Naish now felt that another issue needed to be explored. 'The more we got into it, the more I began to realise that the other really key issue in Australian politics was the integrity piece. And I worked out pretty quickly that one of the reasons we didn't have proper climate policy in Australia was because we didn't have proper integrity in parliament.'

So the group organised another virtual town hall meeting, this time with integrity campaigner and barrister Anthony Whealy, for October. More people watched it and joined Voices of Wentworth.

In November, Sharma tweeted out a *Guardian* article about the rise of independent candidates, saying that 'these so-called independents only target Coalition seats. Is it because they are really "Voices of Labor"?'

The tweet backfired. More than 400 people told him exactly what was wrong with Coalition policies and reminded him that Tasmanian independent Andrew Wilkie had actually taken a Labor seat. Delia Burrage noticed an almost immediate upturn in traffic to the Voices of Wentworth website, with many more people signing up as supporters.

'People are seeing that there's a fundamental disconnect between what the electorate wants and what their representative is doing in parliament,' Burrage told *Crikey*. 'It's not enough to look at what they do in the electorate – Tony Abbott was a volunteer at the local surf club. We think that it's the MP's voting record that they need to be judged on.'[13]

The following month, Atkinson went to an event organised by the Coalition for Conservation, a conservative environmental group, held at the harbourside apartment of chair Cristina Talacko. Matt Kean and Dave Sharma attended, and during the speeches Kean called on the Wentworth MP to do something concrete about climate change, to which Sharma gave vague responses.

Atkinson hadn't known Sharma would be there; it felt odd to be so close to someone she'd been actively planning to remove from his seat. 'I remember feeling like the assassin in the room.'

The search for candidates

In early 2021, the members of Voices of North Sydney faced the inevitable conundrum – should they try to roll the current member at the next election? Most of the members said no, so the activists needed to form a separate group. Although the date of the election was at least a year away, time was now of the essence. Without the infrastructure of the existing parties, the activists had to get cracking in order to build a campaign from the ground up. It's a huge job. About eight local residents including Denise Shrivell and Kristen Lock formed North Sydney's Independent with one main aim: to find a candidate. They started taking donations, created a volunteer roster, completed some early polling and wrote a plan.

Shrivell has extensive networks. A long-time friend of Voices of Goldstein co-founder Sue Barrett, she gave the Victorian her encouragement and advice on how to find a candidate and later helped out the co-founder of Curtin Independent, Tony Fairweather. She credits Twitter as being one of her best recruitment tools.

The new year brought a fresh impetus to all the campaigns. In January, Palese and Atkinson met with several potential candidates; before each discussion, both sides signed non-disclosure agreements. This stopped information leaking out about the plan and also maintained the confidentiality of the women who were interviewed – Palese and Atkinson had already decided that the candidate would be a woman for reasons of strategic advantage and equity.

The following month, Lyndell Droga and Maria Atkinson met up in Palm Beach and joined forces; Wentworth Independents was born (they shortened it to the WIndies).

Cathy McGowan, now retired from politics, continued to be extremely generous with her time and advice. At the end of February, she hosted a 'How to get Elected' two-day seminar on Zoom. Organisers had expected a small number of people to tune in, but 300 people from 81 electorates attended to hear from McGowan and a host of people about becoming an independent candidate.

In the Northern Beaches, Sophie Scamps and Anyo Geddes came to the same realisation as the team in North Sydney – that there was a need for a separate organisation from the Voices group to seek out and support an independent candidate. Accordingly, the women created Mackellar Rising.

In the first week in March, Gold returned to the Eastern Suburbs, bringing with her Tina Jackson, an economist and former CEO of the National Trust, who had been in charge of the Warringah volunteers in 2019. Sitting around Atkinson's dining room table, the two Warringah women laid out a 'six-point plan' for Atkinson, Droga, Palese and Richter on how to emulate their success. After Gold and Jackson left, the other four sat back, their heads reeling. Could they do this?

The woman question

On the morning of International Women's Day, 8 March 2021, the Member for Wentworth stood at Edgecliff railway station and handed out wilted zinnias to women commuters.

A week later, on 15 March, about 110,000 people in forty cities and towns across Australia rallied to call for action on gender equity. The Women's March for Justice protests were triggered by the federal government's lack of response to the alleged sexual assault of Liberal staffer Brittany Higgins in 2019, which was first reported a month before. Scott Morrison refused to attend the march or meet with a representative to discuss the issues; instead, he said in parliament that 'not far from here, such marches even now are being met with bullets, but not here in this country'.

On 27 March, *The Guardian*'s political editor Katharine Murphy published a column about the PM in which she said: 'Let me share a basic insight about Morrison that you might find useful. This prime minister speaks almost exclusively to one cohort of voters: men at risk of voting Labor.'[14]

Polling commissioned by *The Guardian* the following month showed that after months of damaging news about the Coalition's attitudes towards women triggered by the mishandling of Higgins' rape allegations, women were turning their backs on the government, with fewer than one in three giving it their vote.[15]

'It wasn't good enough, and it's not okay for the prime minister to say we want women to succeed but not at the expense of men or that women protesting outside Parliament House are lucky not to be met by bullets,' Naish told me. 'Things like that were just extraordinarily incendiary. And yes, I think that just galvanised women; it was like a catalyst.'

It's impossible not to notice that all these community organisations were created and run by women. Naish explained: 'I think one of the reasons is that women tend to collaborate very strongly together. We all recognised on some intrinsic level that our children are at risk. And we came together so naturally. There are all these like-minded women who were very smart, often professionals but not always, and we had worked very hard and we'd had some level of financial stability and, to be honest, very supportive partners.

'We're all sort of motivated by the same thing, which is to make things better, and we have an inherent understanding that it's not going to happen unless we put ourselves on the line, actually, and demand better. No one's going to deliver it for us.'

Friends in high places

On 19 April, in a speech to the Business Council of Australia, Morrison said, 'We're not going to achieve net zero in the cafes, dinner parties and wine bars of our inner cities.'[16] Every Voices group tucked this quote away to turn into an election ad.

At the end of March, Droga and Atkinson set up for a crucial meeting. Placing water glasses around Droga's dining room table, they mentally rehearsed the upcoming pitch, knowing it could make or break their mission. Both women had had stellar careers – Droga had been a very successful head of philanthropy at the Sydney Opera House and Atkinson was awarded an Order of Australia for being 'a leader and contributor to environmentally sustainable building development in Australia'. But they had never run an election campaign.

Through their networks, the two had learned of communications company Populares and met principal Ed Coper. His business partner, Anthony Reed, had worked on Kerryn Phelps' campaign in 2018 and Steggall's in 2019 – both winners. The Wentworth Independents wanted to hire Populares, but they knew there were other groups in Wentworth who were out looking for a candidate. It was imperative that the WIndies convince Coper and Reed that they represented the best chance of winning the seat.

The two men turned up and the four talked for about an hour, snacking on pistachio nuts while trying to determine if they were the right fit. At the end of the meeting, they agreed to work together and a fixed monthly fee was agreed on. From that date, they met weekly.

The WIndies also engaged a market research company and an advertising agency to create an avatar of the ideal candidate and do a marketing plan. Droga rang a friend, Jessica Block, a former lawyer who now worked in arts administration and philanthropy.

'You know every clever woman in Sydney,' Droga told Block. 'Who do you know would want to stand as an independent candidate in Wentworth?' Block started thinking.

On 13 May, Atkinson arrived early for another crucial meeting, this time with Blair Palese. They'd chosen the private room at Lotus The Galeries restaurant in Sydney's CBD because it was very close to the Hilton Hotel, where the Smart Energy Summit had taken place that day. As they waited, feeling apprehensive, the two women double-checked the seating plan. Invitees were Coper, Reed, John Grimes and Wayne Smith from the Smart Energy Council, and the guests of honour, Simon Holmes à Court and Byron Fay from Climate 200, all of whom had attended the summit.

Atkinson had not met the Climate 200 pair, who had been invited by Grimes and Smith. She was keen to make a good impression – Climate 200 would only fund one independent candidate in each electorate, and she again wanted to make sure their group was chosen. To minimise interruptions, the consultant had pre-ordered the banquet menu and the wine; as the lazy susan rotated and people helped themselves to plates of delicious Shanghainese food, the conversation flowed.

The group talked about politics, international affairs and action on climate change, but there was no overt pitch or formal request for help; both sides were sizing each other up. However, when they were saying their goodbyes, Smith said in an aside that the evening had gone well and that he'd talk to Holmes à Court. 'We'll make sure this is happening for you.'

In June, Droga and the Atkinson-Josephs put $50,000 each into a private company, with an agreement that they would go up to $100,000 if needed. As they were concerned it still may not be enough, they decided to look for one more partner. Droga called her friend Alexa Haslingden, who said that her hands were full with her current project, a women's refuge, but that she'd tell her husband because 'this is more up David's alley than mine'.

The co-owner of RACAT, a group of television production companies, David Haslingden trained as a lawyer before moving to the US to work in broadcasting, ending up the chief operating officer of Fox Networks Group.

Droga called and organised to take Coper and Reed to a meeting with the Haslingdens at RACAT's headquarters: an airy, three-storey warehouse in the inner-city suburb of Redfern. A few days later, they signed up.

In June, North Sydney's Independent held a launch at the Crows Nest Hotel and publicly announced that they were looking for a candidate to run in the next federal election. The group also placed a full-page ad in the *North Shore Times* calling for nominations.

One name put forward was that of charity CEO Kylea Tink. The former CEO of the breast cancer charity the McGrath Foundation and the children's cancer charity Camp Quality, Tink had grown up in the regional NSW town of Coonabarabran. She told the committee that she had voted Liberal in the past.

Later that month, Sydney went into a major lockdown for four months. During this time there were very few reasons for a person to be legally outside their home, the main ones being buying food and taking exercise in groups of two or as a household. The committee members of North Sydney's Independent interviewed Tink during 'walking meetings' around the electorate's parks.

Meanwhile in Wentworth, Jessica Block had an idea. She called Allegra Spender, whom she'd met when Spender was chair of the Sydney Renewable Power Company.

At the time, Spender was the CEO of the Australian Business and Community Network, a group of more than 200 low socio-economic status schools and over forty businesses that worked together to address educational disadvantage. Spender loved her job, which had become even more important during lockdown as the students struggled with accessing resources for remote learning. Spender's mother, Carla Zampatti, had died only a few months earlier, on 3 April. Carla's family had been very close and they were all grief-stricken by her death. But she was also a professional role model. 'The big thing for mum was about women standing up and being courageous and having a go – she really backed women,' Spender told me.

When Block mentioned to her the possibility of running, Spender laughed out loud. But her interest had been piqued, and she decided to seek advice from Jillian Broadbent. The economist had spent thirty years at the highest levels of banking before joining the boards of the Reserve Bank and the Australian Stock Exchange, the Clean Energy Finance Corporation and many other blue-chip Australian companies. Broadbent had been a long-time friend of Zampatti and known Spender since she was a girl.

The biggest issue was that Spender and her husband, technology executive Mark Capps, had three young children, then aged five, eight and nine. She told Broadbent that given the children's ages, she didn't think this was the right time. Broadbent emphasised to the younger woman that there was never a 'right time' for combining career with motherhood.

Spender also spoke to Professor John Daley, founding CEO of the Grattan Institute think tank, who she knew well. She wanted to know if he thought an independent could make a difference. It just so happened that Daley was in the process of finalising a report called *Gridlock*, which envisaged a crucially important role for independent politicians. He was encouraging.

A few days later, Spender rang Droga and suggested a meeting which, due to lockdown, had to be taken on the run. The two women met in their activewear and walked briskly around Centennial Park, weaving around the cavoodles and prams while clutching take-away coffees.

Spender listened to Droga's pitch but again said it was not the right time. 'I said the major barriers were family, work, and even a sense of making sure I'm the right person because I'm conscious that people would perceive me as just being the daughter of someone. I think you have to stand on your own two feet and I felt that could be damaging to the cause.'

Spender had instinctively grasped what the role would entail, Droga told me. 'With her family background, two hard-working full-time working parents, and a dad and grandfather who had been involved in politics at a very high level, she knew what [the candidate] was in for; she knew what to expect.

'And I think she just had an immediate understanding of what the role would be. But having young kids and a job that she loved and all those other things; you see it was a bit of a hurdle for her at the beginning.'

Droga was undaunted, feeling that a door had been opened; Spender didn't say 'no' but only 'not now'. But just in case, the team kept looking.

They'd ruled out approaching women in their thirties because they were too young and lacked life experience; also it was the decade when many women were starting their families. Women in their forties had often gone back to work and were consolidating their careers. Women in their fifties might now be in very senior positions, earning large salaries and generally not having to put up with that much crap; these women were appalled at the standards of behaviour in federal politics and were not interested in being part of it. Other women in their fifties were looking for board positions after retiring from corporate life; if they put up their hands for office and failed to get in, that could rule them out. Another issue was money – Wentworth is the richest electorate in the country, so for many a backbencher's $212,000 salary was a substantial pay cut.

They were looking for a woman 'who could afford to lose and wasn't scared to lose', in Droga's words.

Through a long July of cold, rain and ongoing lockdown, the WIndies were becoming despondent – finding a candidate was becoming a much bigger challenge than they had expected. The team met for walks in the park in front of the Double Bay ferry wharf, discussing this seemingly hopeless quest over Negronis in paper cups. It was a nerve-racking time because there was constant talk that Morrison could call an election before Christmas.

Spender was still mulling over the offer, going on long hikes to gather her thoughts. One regular walk was accompanying Jillian Broadbent along Sydney's eastern coastline from Bondi to Waverley Cemetery. There they would stop and tend to

Zampatti's grave, placing a branch of white magnolias, her favourite flowers, next to the headstone.

Spender asked the businesswoman for advice, and Broadbent told her it was the perfect role for her. She also pointed out that after doing a job like this, Spender could go into all sorts of policy institutions. The door would open on a much bigger picture.

Droga kept Spender up to speed with their progress. She recalled that Spender could see the movement growing. 'We had another one of our Zoom [discussions] with over 400 people watching and she was watching, as was John Spender.'

At the end of July, the Teals received a morale boost when the Grattan Institute published the *Gridlock* report, which examined the barriers to policy reform in Australia.[17] The report concluded that 'the most likely prospect for institutional change is that independent members of parliament demand it as the price of their support when they hold the balance of power or their votes are needed to pass legislation. A drive for institutional changes is likely to fit with the electoral platform and political self-interest of cross-benchers'.

The following month, Holmes à Court relaunched Climate 200, which had been in hibernation following the 2019 election. He presented his 'root and branch model' for campaign financing at the WIndies Zoom fundraiser event for potential donors. Reed presented the research they'd had done by a marketing company, and Atkinson and Palese also spoke.

When one woman kicked off the discussion and put her hand up for a donation, it prompted a flood of offers which soon reached a total of $69,000. At the end of the meeting, without warning, Holmes à Court jumped in to say that Climate 200 would match the money, bringing the total to almost $140,000. A good night's work.

The Liberals get nervous

In the Northern Beaches, the Voices of Mackellar group released the *Mackellar Matters Report* in August, and shared it with the current federal, state and local representatives. The report described the top five concerns of the participants, which were the need for stronger action on climate change along with concerns about threats to the local environment and the power of political lobbyists and donors, the need for a federal integrity commission, and the problems of growing inequality.[18] Following the report's release, the group hosted a number of events and panel discussions on these topics of major concern.

The Liberal Party had obviously done some polling in Mackellar and discovered that Falinski was in trouble. In early September, instead of trying to address the community group's concerns, they started treating it as a combination of the Khmer Rouge and the CFMMEU.

Falinski had declined to attend a Voices of Mackellar event on the grounds that it was a 'political rally', which would have been 'inappropriate' for him to attend. He labelled groups such as Voices of Mackellar 'left wing front groups' that were 'the next chapter in the book of GetUp!'[19]

Senator Andrew Bragg then asked the Australian Electoral Commission to investigate the Voices groups because, according to an article in the *Northern Beaches Advocate*, they had 'an agenda to unseat Coalition members of parliament, with Voices of Warringah widely credited with boosting Zali Steggall's campaign to defeat former Prime Minister Tony Abbott'.[20]

Kylea Tink publicly announced her candidature for North Sydney on 18 September, saying her number one concern was action on climate change. She told *The Sydney Morning Herald* that the government was 'protecting the VHS economy while everyone else has moved onto the livestream economy'.[21]

North Sydney's Independent was greatly encouraged by the results of Climate 200–commissioned polling done before Tink was announced showing that 16 per cent of voters in the seat said they would give their first preference to an unnamed independent. The electorate was hungry for change.

Meanwhile, in Wentworth, the WIndies were convinced that Spender was the right person, but she was still saying 'Now is not the right time.'

She didn't have just her husband and children to consider. Spender's brother Alex Schuman was the chief executive of the Carla Zampatti fashion business and her sister Bianca Spender owned her eponymous fashion label. Both companies were very successful, but overt political affiliations could affect that. The three siblings are very close, and Spender consulted them about the decision.

Schuman had worked for former NSW Premier Gladys Berejiklian for five years, so any decision would affect his political connections. Spender recalled that her brother told her, 'If you do it, I'll support you, even if the Liberal Party scratches their head.' Both Bianca and John Spender urged caution at first, mindful of the difficulties of a politician's life. But once they realised Allegra was serious, they gave their total support. Although John's ongoing respiratory issues meant that he was unable to attend any public events during Allegra's campaign, he often gave her advice, while both Alex and Bianca went to events and worked hard for the campaign behind the scenes.

In the first two weeks of November, Morrison attended the COP26 global environmental conference in Glasgow. His speech to the conference received a withering assessment from the Climate Council: 'Prime Minister Scott Morrison has addressed world leaders at COP26 in Glasgow with a speech that was light on commitments and credibility, but heavy on spin ... Our actions so far at COP26 have only cemented our global reputation as a climate action blocker.'[22]

In the end, COP26 was the final straw for Spender.

'I had a little mental model in my head, which was like, if they do something decent on COP26, then I won't move,' she told me. 'But when they came out with no additional target to 2030, and it was clear that Barnaby Joyce basically sets the agenda for Australia's climate action, I was so disappointed ... And so I just thought, "Someone has to do this."'[23]

Spender rang Droga and said yes.

It was the hardest decision she'd ever made and there were a few sleepless nights. But despite the potential impact on her family, Spender knew 'you have to show your kids and particularly girls that when things are worth doing, you can find ways through it, and that's totally what Mum showed me'.

In the last week of November, the Drogas woke up to the unwelcome news that they had been the target of a negative article in *The Australian Financial Review*.[24] The story portrayed them as wealthy dilettantes, and focused on the types of shares in Daniel's funds management business and an estimated value of their Woollahra home. The smiling photo included was taken when they and other Droga family members donated $1 million for an Indigenous architecture scholarship at the University of Technology, Sydney. But placed next to the story, the photo made them look smug and self-satisfied.

A few people who had agreed to donate now asked to do so anonymously because they wanted to avoid the same fate.

Lyndell Droga was devastated. 'It's a lesson – don't put your head up, because guess what's going to happen? That stops a whole lot of people participating; it stops them publicly saying they're going to be supportive, donating, publicly coming to events, hosting events, all of the above by seeing how some people get treated … That's what they're trying to do: send a signal.'

A few days later, Spender's campaign was launched at the Paddington RSL. Despite the unceasing rain, 600 people turned up. Jillian Broadbent introduced the candidate, saying that the only negative thing she had ever heard Zampatti say about Allegra was that she had absolutely no interest in fashion. At the time, Broadbent had remonstrated with her old friend: 'But she is studying economics at Cambridge!'

Sophie Scamps launched her election campaign on 5 December in Avalon, telling a huge crowd that her number one priority was addressing climate change 'and definitely not waiting until 2050 when it will be too late. The world – is telling us. Our children are telling us. Even the Business Council of Australia is telling us'.[25]

It was a call to action. By election day, her campaign had more than 1200 volunteers.

Spender was keen to start campaigning seriously, but the new year got off to a slow start when members of her household took turns to test positive to Omicron, keeping her in isolation for about three weeks. Once the new candidate could leave the house, she started going out into the community to connect with local groups. Spender went to police stations, homeless shelters, women's refuges, church soup kitchens, community groups – basically anywhere she was invited. There, she asked endless questions and listened, intently.

The WIndies started having regular 'meet the candidate' events in private homes around the Eastern Suburbs, where Spender would give a short speech and answer questions. One of the attendees, a prominent banker, had been taken along by his wife. He grilled the candidate on the economics of renewable energy and came away impressed with the extent of her knowledge. The fundraising element was not overt, but the money flowed in. Once people had had the chance to meet Spender, many were converted.

In February, Spender was a guest on the satirical *Betoota Advocate Podcast* and spoke about the Liberal Party of today being very different to the party to which her father and grandfather belonged. 'I think we need to come back to some of the values that the Liberal Party used to espouse, and you look at what [Malcolm] Fraser did in terms of how he welcomed refugees. And you say, well, these are really different qualities and different values to the ones that we're seeing right now.'[26]

On 5 March, the Sydney Gay and Lesbian Mardi Gras ended with a COVID-safe parade around the Sydney Cricket Ground in Moore Park. Wentworth is the electorate with the highest number of LGBTQI+ people in the country and Spender and many of her fellow NSW Teal candidates were there, as was Sharma.

As the two had never met, Spender went over to introduce herself. She thanked the MP for the note he had written following her mother's death, and he responded by saying that she had spoken beautifully at the funeral.

'We tried to keep it civil,' she told me. 'There's no point in it being personal. It's not easy, and I have a lot of personal sympathy for what it's like to lose your seat publicly because I remember what it was like when my dad lost his seat – it's not easy for your family.'

On 11 March, Sharma put out teal-coloured election material, indicating to everyone that the Liberals really were concerned about the seat. It was more good publicity for his opponent.

At his campaign launch on 27 March, Sharma told supporters that he was 'not doing this as a mid-life frolic, or as a hobby, or as a vanity project. I'm not here because of who my parents are, or where I went to school'.[27] The professional women in the electorate heard that dog-whistle.

Malcolm Turnbull told *The Sydney Morning Herald* that the rise of small-l liberal independents was an understandable reaction to the federal Liberals 'being seen as too right-wing on most issues', particularly climate change. The former PM said the attempt to characterise the independent movement as a Labor Party front was 'an insult to people's intelligence'.

'The challenge the Liberal Party faces is no matter how reasonable its individual candidates may be, if the party is not seen to represent the values of a large section of what had hitherto been their regular traditional voters, those voters will look for alternatives.'[28]

On 5 April, *The Australian* newspaper published a hit-job on Blair Palese, accusing her of anti-Semitism on social media.[29] This was the kind of accusation that could lose the Spender campaign the election. According to the 2016 census, 12.5 per cent of the Wentworth electorate identified as Jewish, making them a crucial voting bloc. Any serious candidate had to demonstrate a connection to the community; Sharma was put into the seat because he'd been Australia's ambassador to Israel.

It's widely thought that the Jewish community votes conservatively, but this is a generalisation; they have as many different views as any other group. But the constant whispers about the Spender campaign being anti-Semitic had been damaging and difficult to counter.

Three days after *The Australian*'s story, the two Wentworth candidates faced off for a debate at Moriah College, a prominent Jewish school in the electorate.

Spender addressed the elephant in the room. She described Palese as an 'early supporter of Wentworth Independents' and 'an expert in climate issues, so I spoke to her a couple of times about climate change. I did not know her views on [boycotts] and Israel because we never discussed them'. Spender confirmed her support for 'the existence of a strong Israel which has the right to self-defence while it pursues its two-state solution'.[30]

In North Sydney, Tink put out a strongly-worded critique of Morrison's 2022 budget, saying that climate action and political integrity were almost entirely neglected. 'There was almost no evidence of any movement towards net zero, with more support going to gas and petrol than renewables and EVs', she wrote in a newsletter. This budget was 'another display of short-termism and marketing tricks.'

Up in Mackellar, the Scamps team was greatly encouraged by the results of a UComms poll. When asked, 23.9% of the voters said that they would give their first preferences to Scamps, with 35.2% voting for Falinski. This meant that the final result would be very close and go to preferences.

* * *

On 10 April, the government called the election for 21 May, making it a six-week campaign.

All three NSW candidates started the campaign in good shape. They each had hundreds of volunteers, high name recognition in the community and cash in the bank. What they didn't have, at least according to the polls, was a clear path to victory.

3.

A DIFFERENT FRONT: VICTORIA AND WESTERN AUSTRALIA

The three Teals in Victoria and Western Australia – Dr Monique Ryan in Kooyong, Zoe Daniel in Goldstein and Kate Chaney in Curtin – were in a different position to their NSW counterparts. Instead of facing off against moderate Liberals, they faced a less predictable type of opponent.

Although the Liberal Party assumed that Josh Frydenberg was personally popular, qualitative polling revealed that wasn't the case. His strident criticism of Victorian premier Daniel Andrews over the pandemic lockdowns offended many voters, who perceived it as playing political games during a health crisis.

The politics of Goldstein's Tim Wilson lean towards the libertarian, free-speech side of the Liberal Party. A former policy director at the right-wing Institute of Public Affairs think tank, he has said he has an 'open mind' regarding the science behind climate change.[31] Despite being in a same-sex marriage, he also defended the rights of religious groups to discriminate against LGBTQI+ people and was one of the MPs who argued for the repeal of Section 18C (racial vilification) of the *Racial Discrimination Act*.

Over in Western Australia, Chaney was the only Teal who faced a female candidate, which made it more challenging to campaign on gender-related issues. But the member for Curtin, Celia Hammond, was not a member of the sisterhood. A conservative Catholic who raised concerns in a 2013 speech about 'premarital casual sex' and 'militant feminism', she was also on record as downplaying the extent of humanity's contribution to global warming and refused to reveal how she voted in the same-sex marriage survey.

Theoretically, Ryan, Daniel and Chaney should have had an easier job than their NSW counterparts. But nothing is that simple. This chapter is shorter than the last one, which covered many of the common issues relating to the electorates and the campaigns, like the bushfires and the effects of the pandemic.

Melbourne mobilises

In early 2020, Goldstein resident Sue Barrett watched the unfolding nightmare of the Black Summer bushfires in despair. The business strategist and her friends started looking for ways to create real change, reasoning that if the government wouldn't do anything, they needed to mobilise and take back control. Barrett herself recognised the pattern here. 'If you pardon the pun, I believe this crisis lit the fuse for many and kick-started community action.'

Together with the Bayside Climate Crisis Action Group, Barrett and others had been speaking to local member Tim Wilson about action on climate change, to no avail. 'Many Goldstein voters told us how deeply frustrated they were with Wilson, the career politician who always voted with Barnaby and simply didn't give a stuff about us. We'd had enough.'

Barrett was in regular contact with an old friend, media executive Denise Shrivell in North Sydney. For years they'd been talking about emulating Cathy McGowan and finding a community independent candidate to run in their seats. They now started talking in earnest.

In January 2021, Barrett and her colleagues founded Voices of Goldstein with one aim: to do democracy better. After holding a number of public meetings, they decided that the best way to achieve that was to support a community independent candidate at the 2022 election.

Together, the group developed the Goldstein Standard, a set of values and principles to guide the group and any future candidate. They set out core values – respect, integrity, inclusivity and positivity – and the members committed to being their best selves; being kind, compassionate and welcoming; listening respectfully and learning from others; and engaging constructively.

Voices of Goldstein created a website and social media accounts, and started conducting Kitchen Table Conversations. At their first public meeting in April, 'How to Win Back Our Democracy', former Liberal leader John Hewson spoke along with Steggall, McGowan and writer and comedian Craig Reucassel, who had directed a documentary about campaign financing called *Big Deal: Is Our Democracy for Sale?*

In early April, the group approached the former member for Goldstein, Ian Macphee, to gauge his potential support. A moderate Liberal, he had crossed the floor in 1984 to vote for Labor's *Sex Discrimination Act*.

During an interview, Macphee said, 'I believe grassroots activity is imperative and can be done by supporting good independent candidates.'[32]

In a message of support for Voices of Goldstein, he elaborated: 'The more independent Senators and Members of the House of Representatives we can have to review policies and their implementation, the better – that's the state we have got to in our democracy which has been abused by power hungry people.'[33]

Voices of Goldstein assembled a candidate selection panel of six local residents, three men and three women, aged from their twenties to their eighties, from across the political spectrum. Advertisements for the position of candidate were placed on social media in June.

A few weeks later, journalist and TV presenter Angela Pippos had an idea. She didn't know Barrett or how to contact her, so she messaged her on Twitter. They exchanged phone numbers and Pippos called, telling Barrett, 'I think my best friend Zoe Daniel would be ideal.'

When the three of them met later that month, Barrett raised the idea of Daniel running as an independent. The former ABC foreign correspondent was shocked. 'Not a chance in hell!' she exclaimed. But Barrett asked if they could stay in touch and Daniel agreed.

Could it happen in WA?

Over in Fremantle, it was a glorious spring day and Tony Fairweather was sitting at his favourite cafe. On opening his laptop and reading the news, his interest was piqued by a story on Zali Steggall's proposed climate change bills. He read further, finding out more detail about her famous 2019 victory over former PM Tony Abbott in Warringah.[34]

That night the solicitor lay in bed, sleepless, thinking about the parallels with Curtin.

The inner-metropolitan Perth electorate stretches from the Indian Ocean to the Swan River and contains Perth's most affluent suburbs. Residents of two of them, Cottesloe and Peppermint Grove, have just been named as Australia's wealthiest, with an annual average taxable income of $325,000. As with Warringah, the electorate had a high number of well-educated voters who wanted strong action on climate change and had voted 'yes' in the same-sex marriage survey.

Former Liberal deputy leader Julie Bishop had held the seat for twenty-one years until her retirement from politics in 2019, after which it had been subject to one of the vicious, prolonged pre-selection battles that have lately come to define the modern Liberal Party. The eventual winner, legal academic Celia Hammond, was backed by The Clan, the dominant right-wing faction of the Western Australian Liberals. In a 2019 interview with *The Australian*, she said that humanity's contribution to climate change is 'very minimal'.[35] A conservative Catholic, she has declined to say how she voted in the same-sex marriage survey.

Hammond said during the 2022 campaign that her views had changed, 'but I'm still fundamentally the same person, and I don't actually label myself anything. So when it was put to me that I was conservative as opposed to moderate, my response is – I'm a Liberal'.[36]

The academic was not popular in Curtin – there had been an 11.3 per cent swing against her in 2019; post-redistribution, her margin fell to 13.9 per cent. Tellingly, Bishop neither endorsed the Liberal candidate nor assisted her campaign.

Fairweather knew there was a fundamental mismatch between Hammond and the socially progressive profile of Curtin. He calculated that an independent needed to drag Hammond's primary vote below 45 per cent and then run second in order to receive preferences from Labor and the Greens to win in 2022.

A few days later Fairweather was back at the same cafe when lawyer Sarah Silbert came in. The two knew each other through their children's school; when she asked what he was doing, he half-jokingly replied, 'I am trying to create Australian political history.'

A few weeks later, Silbert joined Fairweather and three more friends around a kitchen table, where they thrashed out the values of Curtin and wrote it all down. However, they knew they were in dire need of help. Neither of the two lawyers had any political experience, and besides, it was now close to Christmas. Time was of the essence.

Fairweather then had a lucky break. After speaking to Michael Ottaviano, a former neighbour, he discovered that Michael's wife Mandy was involved with the North Sydney's Independent campaign. Mandy quickly connected Fairweather with Kristen Lock and Denise Shrivell, who generously shared their expertise. 'We were way behind our sister electorates in ... Kooyong, Goldstein and Mackellar, who were already on the ground and running hard. We had no time to waste.'[37] The Western Australians drew up a plan for action, and Curtin Independent was up and running.

The candidates come on board

Meanwhile, Voices of Goldstein had spent three months whittling down the pool to a few suitable candidates. During this time Sue Barrett kept checking in with Zoe Daniel to see if she had changed her mind about running. The group decided that in case Morrison called an early election they needed to finalise the candidate selection by the end of October. Barrett called Daniel to check one last time, and, to her delight, the former journalist said she would 'like to throw her hat in the ring'.

Daniel was not given a free ride – she had to go through the same selection processes as the other potential candidates. She won. Now the campaign could begin.

A bit further north in Melbourne's eastern suburbs, in Kooyong, retired academic Ann Capling was getting frustrated. She was part of a Facebook group called Kew 3101 which had originally focused on the local council but during lockdown had pivoted to bigger political issues, particularly climate change. Capling, an expert on the international political economy, and thirty other residents decided to merge the membership of Kew 3101 and another group to form Voices of Kooyong.

Capling then approached Oliver Yates to ask if she could use the infrastructure of Kooyong Independents, the group that had supported his candidature in 2019 when the renewable energy executive ran against Frydenberg and won 9 per cent of the primary vote. The dormant group had a database of 600 people and access to the NationBuilder software, which political candidates can use to create a website and facilitate donations. Yates agreed.

Frydenberg was vulnerable; his constant attacks on Victorian premier Dan Andrews over lockdowns had hurt his popularity. Capling told *The Age*: 'We were all really stuck at home. We didn't have jobs to go to. People were trying really hard in that lockdown and it was like he was just pissing on the community effort.'[38]

Kooyong Independents took out full-page advertisements in *The Age* and *The Australian Financial Review* on 20 October, headlined, 'Are You the Next Member for Kooyong?'

One person who read that headline was Dr Monique Ryan.

The fifty-four-year-old paediatric neurologist was employed at the Royal Children's Hospital Melbourne. She was also part of a research group based at the Murdoch Children's Research Institute and was a full-time clinician, meaning that she saw patients from newborns to eighteen-year-olds. Just before reading the ad, she had acted as head of the department of neurology for six weeks, replacing someone on holiday. There, she discovered that she had a desire for working on a bigger canvas.

Ryan told me that when she saw the ad, 'It made me laugh actually, because I thought, that's a good idea … I hope they find someone good.'

But a couple of friends sent the ad to her as well, saying she should do it. 'And I guess that's what made me think about it.'

Ryan said that initially she didn't think that she was the right person for the job. 'I knew I could do the job if I was elected to do it, but the chances of that were much less than someone in the public eye like Zoe Daniel.'

However, she acknowledged that the thought of running 'wasn't completely out of the blue'. She said that she'd become increasingly frustrated with the government's inaction on climate change, attitudes to gender equity and lack of transparency in decision-making, adding that she thought there had been a 'toxic miasma of dishonesty and corruption' hanging over the Morrison government.

'I was invested in Australian politics, but it was really just a sense of rising desperation and feeling that someone really needed to do that and that if I felt like that, that I should consider putting my own hand up.'

Ryan applied online, answering a question about the most embarrassing thing she'd ever done – coming second on TV quiz show *Sale of the Century* (a skateboard and a cot were

the prizes). But she failed to reveal perhaps the most contentious thing she'd ever done, which was hold a Labor Party
membership for three years. When asked by *The Age* if she
had any political experience, she answered, 'No, nothing. I am
a complete cleanskin.'[39] When her membership leaked out
during the campaign, the Liberals used it against her.

In mid-November, Ryan met Oliver Yates for a coffee.
'And the first thing I said to him was, look, I'm not the right
person for this, I'm sure you can find someone better. But then
I found myself trying to convince him that I was the right
person. At the end of it he said I should do it because the reality
is that it was a fantastic adventure.'

A few weeks later, she met with Capling and a colleague
and also Simon Holmes à Court, who later stressed that he
attended in the capacity of a concerned local resident, not as
the convenor of Climate 200. Capling told *The Age*, 'We'd all
looked at Monique's application and we thought she was politi-
cally very inexperienced, but she just gave us a little shiver.'[40]

It's not hard to see why the panel liked her; Ryan radiates
a poised, no-nonsense competence born of years managing
life-and-death situations. She told me that during stressful
events like attending a cardiac arrest, she deliberately slows
down and calms herself so she can act effectively. In fact, this
was demonstrated a couple of times during pre-poll when
people collapsed inside the voting booth; although candidates
are technically not allowed inside these areas, they made an
exception for the doctor (all survived).

Ryan was asked to submit a written plan for how she'd
win the election. In it, she used an analogy from her experience dealing with young people with chronic pain. 'A lot of
adolescents have headaches that affect them every single day
and they miss school and they end up dropping out of school or

having to repeat. And I basically said [in my plan] sometimes you just have to change the language. I say to those kids, "Look, it's excellent news, you haven't got a brain tumour, you can get better from this. It's going to take a bit of discipline and resolution and it's not going to happen overnight, but we can do it."'

She explained that activists needed to change the language about climate change and see it as an opportunity and talk about it in a positive way, because most people are frightened of it. 'And most people when they get frightened, they freeze.'

The campaign group told her they'd decided the candidate had to be a woman; the candidates for the three main parties in Kooyong were all male, so it would be fairer and also advantageous to have a woman.

Ryan said she had a few discussions with her husband, health products executive Peter Jordan. 'The issue was, if I had said to him, "I'm going to go and do this for six months and then I'll go back to my real job", he would have said, "Absolutely no problem, of course, go for gold". But I was actually saying "I need to go off and do this for six months and at the end of it, who knows?"' In the end, Jordan told her, 'Obviously you need to do this.'

On 25 November, Zoe Daniel was announced as the community independent candidate for Goldstein to a crowd of more than 600 people at the Sandringham Rotunda.

Daniel told them she was a swinging voter who had never been a member of a political party. But she voted Liberal in 2016 largely because she supported the then-prime minister, Malcolm Turnbull, and what she considered to be progressive climate and economic policies. Since Turnbull was 'white-anted' out of office, moderate Liberals such as Tim Wilson had been more interested in supporting the conservative approach of the National Party than representing their electorates, she asserted.

Daniel insisted that it was time Wilson was held accountable. 'It's to do with what they do, not what they say.'

Sue Barrett, now the campaign manager, had started branding their website and social media pages with their messaging, 'Find Your Voice' and 'If Not Us, Who? If Not Now, When?' An hour after Daniel's event, the website went live. Almost immediately, $8000 dropped into the donation box and the social media content went viral. The campaign team had ordered 300 T-shirts for the launch but they sold out in fifteen minutes; one person paid $10,000 for one of the last remaining ones.

At the end of November, Ryan attended an event called 'Australia's Eroding Democracy', hosted by Voices of Kooyong. Capling told the crowd that the candidate would be announced at the launch in two weeks' time.

Afterwards a group went to drinks at Holmes à Court's house, where the entrepreneur told Ryan's husband they thought she had a good chance. 'And I think at that point, it just dawned upon Pete that [Holmes à Court] actually seriously thought that I might win and he thought, "Oh my god, what has she done?"'

On 12 December, Ryan's campaign was launched at the Hawthorn Arts Centre. In her speech, she first emphasised her local roots, and then went on to outline her climate focus.

'I am here – and I suspect you are too – because our current Member for Kooyong is neglecting his responsibilities, and because the problems we face are too serious for any of us to sit on the sidelines anymore. My job has always been to care for our children and to protect their futures. I have increasing concerns about the effects of climate change and our government's inactivity on this front.

'Isn't it time that Kooyong had a representative who understands the urgency of the climate crisis?'[41]

At the end of 2021, Australia went into its usual summer holiday shutdown. All the campaigns that had chosen candidates ramped up their digital advertising campaigns, hoping that people were still paying attention.

In Perth, the members of Curtin Independent weren't observing any shutdowns; they were working around the clock. They had started to look for a candidate, and Kate Chaney's name was put forward.

The Chaneys are a well-known Western Australian dynasty; Kate's father Michael Chaney was the chief executive or chairman of several large public companies, and her uncle Fred Chaney and grandfather Fred Senior were both Liberal frontbenchers. Kate trained as a lawyer before doing an MBA, working at Boston Consulting and, in the Chaney tradition, serving on corporate and philanthropic boards. Married with three children, Chaney looks exactly like her mother Rose, a strikingly attractive woman.

On 4 January, some of the Curtin Independents made a Zoom call to Chaney while she was on a family holiday on Rottnest Island. Later that evening Chaney called Lyndell Droga, who she knew through a mutual friend. She told Droga that she'd been approached to stand and asked for advice. The two women talked for some time.

For Chaney, it was a big call to give up her job at Anglicare WA to run as an independent candidate with no salary, uncertain financial backing and a 13.9 per cent incumbent margin. But she weighed up the decision and ultimately made up her mind quite quickly, notifying the team on 20 January. A week later, her candidature was announced with a front-page story in *The West Australian*.

At the end of the month, *The Saturday Paper* published a story about her by journalist Margo Kingston.[42] Asked about her family pedigree, Chaney bridled: 'I hope it's not just the surname – I'm a bit chippy about that. I'm not a representative of the Chaney family. There's a diverse spectrum of views within my family and I don't know if it's appropriate for my family to come out and give their blessing. It's much more about the community than about them.'

She went on to criticise the party of her uncle and grandfather. 'The Liberal Party is about power without purpose now. What they're good at is the politics – the policies are a whole lot less interesting or important. So it's "get in power and stay in power" rather than actually using that power to achieve anything.'

Chaney said that it was her duty to stand, because many people were not in her fortunate position. 'There's financial risk, there's reputational risk, there's personal cost in terms of family responsibilities.'

The day after Chaney's candidature was announced, the *West Australian* newspaper quoted Julie Bishop as saying she thought that Chaney could win. The former member remained neutral throughout the campaign, again not endorsing Hammond.

At the campaign launch on 6 February, Chaney told a crowd of 300 supporters that she was disillusioned with federal politics. 'I feel like my vote in Curtin is taken for granted. The major parties have moved away from the centre and the policies of Scott Morrison and Barnaby Joyce do not represent the views and values of Curtin.'[43]

She spoke about climate change, integrity and community. 'We are compassionate and socially progressive. And we are not seeing that reflected in our representation.'

She told the crowd, which included Janet Holmes à Court and several members of the Chaney family, that they faced a big challenge. 'The Liberal Party won this electorate with a 54 per cent primary vote in the last election. We've got fourteen weeks. We've got 108,000 people to reach. So we've got a bit of a mountain to climb.'

By election day, there were 860 volunteers.

'This will change politics forever'

In Goldstein, Tim Wilson had decided to fight the election on technicalities rather than issues. In February he claimed publicly that Zoe Daniel's signs had breached council by-laws. 'It is unlawful to erect signs until after the election has been called,' Wilson wrote to his constituents, inviting them to dob in the perpetrators. This instead triggered a wave of donations to Climate 200, who passed along $25,000 to Daniel's campaign.

Bayside City Council kept changing its mind on the issue and ended up threatening to issue $900 fines to people displaying Daniel's corflutes. Chair of Voices of Goldstein, retired accountant Keith Badger, put his house on the line to take the council to the Victorian Supreme Court, winning the case and setting a precedent for laws around political signage.

This triggered more media attention, which generated more donations to Daniel's campaign.

On 10 April, more than a thousand people turned up to the Trey Bit Reserve in Sandringham for the campaign launch. Ian Macphee and former Labor minister Barry Jones had front-row seats. Jones said, 'I've never seen anything like this in my life. It's so exciting and so invigorating. This will change politics forever.'

Daniel addressed the crowd, saying that the Morrison government had stopped governing. 'Report after report delivers recommendations that are not implemented because our major parties won't tackle anything that's hard, they will only do what's popular. And taking the easy option every time to either keep power or get into power will not take us forward as a nation or a community.'[44]

By the time of the election on 21 May, the team of 1500 volunteers had done fifty street meets, door-knocked 44,000 homes, made more than 4000 phone calls and erected more than 2500 fence signs. As Sue Barrett told me, 'Nothing beats organised money like organised people.'

In Kooyong, Monique Ryan attended several community events a day. But she felt she and Frydenberg were running two entirely different campaigns. 'We were swimming in our own lane doing this grassroots thing, getting the corflutes out, people in T-shirts, flyers, stalls, markets – you know, meeting people, talking to people, door-knocking, that sort of stuff,' she recalled. 'He was doing the big picture stuff, the sort of traditional big party stuff, lots and lots of billboards and paid advertising and things like that.

'We couldn't afford to do that, so the paid advertising that we did was much more directed, it was [using] digital media.'

After the election, research hub RMIT FactLab analysed the two campaigns. FactLab, part of RMIT's School of Media and Communication, conducts original research into the digital news ecosystem. The most critical piece of data for the Kooyong campaign was the fact that people aged between 18 and 34 constituted the largest group in the electorate: 26.2 per cent. Because of this, consultants Populares and The RedBridge Group created a positive, digital-first campaign that was in stark contrast to the Liberals' (more on this in chapter 4).

While the independent was critical of the Morrison government's climate policies, she rarely made it personal by attacking her political opponent. Frydenberg often campaigned very negatively, calling Ryan 'my opponent' instead of using her name, and often describing her as a 'fake' or a 'so-called' independent.

On Facebook and Twitter, Frydenberg mainly communicated policies tied to the Morrison government and promoted his record as treasurer, whereas Ryan campaigned strongly on climate action, integrity in politics and gender equality, which were largely absent from Liberal social media. One of the advantages of a digital campaign is that it is much easier to gauge popularity as the engagement statistics are right in front of you. The Liberal posts promoting older, high-profile politicians and football clubs had low levels of engagement, unlike Ryan's community-focused campaign of positive messaging on her three main issues. The digital team made effective use of hashtags to amplify messages. All social media posts were consistently tagged #Mon4Kooyong and #KooyongVotes, with the strategy generating thousands of re-posts and shares across Facebook, Twitter, Instagram and TikTok.

While Ryan's team was running a positive, community-focused campaign that reached the large group of younger electors, the Liberals were placing large banners around the suburbs with the slogan 'Keep Josh'. And many voters thought, 'Why should we?'

* * *

As the election campaign started, the two Victorian electorates were in reasonably good shape for the Teals; the polling looked positive and they had money in the bank.

The Chaney campaign in Western Australia was the odd one out. They didn't start campaigning seriously until the new year and, with a core campaign team of only eight people, were seriously under-resourced. Curtin Independent lacked the funds for polling or sophisticated marketing and the only Perth newspaper, *The West Australian*, owned by billionaire business-man Kerry Stokes, was relentlessly pro-Liberal.

Kate Chaney and her team of political neophytes were trying to take from the Liberal Party its fifth-safest metropoli-tan seat. In February, she said, 'I've no doubt that I'm coming in as the underdog.'[45]

But across the country, nothing felt certain. Climate 200 and their pollster, The Redbridge Group, calculated that if the voting intention numbers stayed on the current trajectory, the first preference votes for the Teals would hit the low-to-mid 20s on election day, which was too low. As the formal election campaign started there were many worried faces – the people behind the campaigns had not come this far and spent this much money to end up second best.

4.

THE DREAM TEAM: CLIMATE 200, POPULARES AND REDBRIDGE

The best part of being an independent candidate is that you can run your own race without having to answer to some controlling party hack in head office. But the downside? You're starting from behind, raising all the money and building the infrastructure by yourself. It's not hard to see why so few independent candidates ever run for parliament, let alone win – it's an almost impossible task. And elections are binary; you don't get a prize for running a 'pretty good' campaign. While success has many fathers (or mothers), failure is an orphan.

The major parties actually get money back after an election. Parties and candidates that receive more than 4 per cent of the primary vote are entitled to public election funding of $3.016 multiplied by the number of votes they receive. This generates millions of dollars for them and tops up their coffers.

Apart from cash, the biggest issue for any independent candidate is lack of access to the knowledge embedded in a political party – decades of expertise on polling, strategy, research and advertising.

For the 2022 election, Simon Holmes à Court found a way to change this situation. He took the group he founded in 2019, Climate 200, and used it to build a war chest from crowd-funded donations. He then assembled a highly experienced group of pollsters, strategists and election experts, including communications group Populares – which included some of the team from Zali Steggall's first winning campaign – and polling group RedBridge, set up by a veteran Labor Party office-holder.

Climate 200: Facilitating change

Climate 200's executive director, public policy expert Byron Fay, said that the group's contribution to the campaigns was money, data and effective communications content.

In 2019, Climate 200 had raised $500,000 from twenty-seven donors in just a few weeks. This time they started their crowdfunding campaign in mid-2021; by election day they'd raised almost $13 million from 11,200 donors. Collectively, Climate 200's contributors come from every electorate in the country, with one-third from rural and regional Australia.

Thirteen million sounds like a lot of money, but it's small change compared to the major parties. In 2019 alone, the ALP raised $126 million and the Coalition $181 million, with Clive Palmer's United Australia Party spending almost $60 million, rising to almost $100 million in 2022.

Timing was everything in fundraising, Fay told me. Most backers try to emulate a group like EMILY's List Australia, which is a financial, political and personal support network for progressive Labor women in Australian politics. 'EMILY' stands for 'Early Money Is Like Yeast' because it makes the dough rise, Fay said. Climate 200 knew that getting money into the coffers of individual groups quite early enabled them to both start their campaigning and also raise more money from the community by making a series of 'matching' challenges.

After Climate 200 started distributing funds, RedBridge commenced a program of qualitative polling. Simon Holmes à Court has said that they did not fund early-stage start-ups, only campaigns they thought had a chance of winning.[46] Fay and his colleagues were happy with the progress of the campaigns – many of the metrics they looked at, such as volunteer numbers, media mentions and community fundraising, were improving. But two months out from the election, the thirty-five-year-old Oxford graduate started to get nervous.

Although the campaigns appeared to be tracking well, the polling wasn't reflecting that. While the percentage of people indicating they would vote for an independent candidate was rising, on the current trajectory by election day the numbers would reach the low to mid 20s, which was not enough. Fay felt that perhaps the community wasn't ready.

'I was quite concerned but there was nothing really we could do about it and we charged on, kept fundraising and kept providing support. [The candidates] kept doing the same, working hard building the community campaign – and then when the election was called [on 10 April] everything changed; it completely, completely exploded.'

In 2020, Fay had worked in the US with a group called Main Street One, which used social media influencers to help inoculate populations against campaign misinformation and then counter it when it appeared. For example, one of the successful campaigns, 'Vote Like A Madre', was aimed at getting Latina women to vote for climate change action.

With this experience under his belt and armed with the data showing 2022 would be the first election in which younger voters combined outnumbered baby boomers, Fay and the

Climate 200 team devised a wildly successful social media campaign. 'It Takes 3' used influencers to spread the message that only three new independent candidates were needed to break the political deadlock and effect real action on climate change, gender equity and integrity in politics; by election day, it had had two million views.

Populares: The persuaders

One of the key players in the Teal story is Populares, which was formed after Ed Coper returned to Australia from New York in early 2020. At that time, he joined up with Mark Connelly and Anthony Reed; Reed had been Kerryn Phelps' campaign manager in the 2018 by-election and went on to run Zali Steggall's successful campaign in Warringah in 2019, while Connelly, a former corporate lawyer, had worked here and in the US.

Coper, a self-described 'changemaker strategist', was at Australian activist group GetUp! before moving to the US to work on Barack Obama's 2012 campaign and social action platform Change.org. He also founded social change agency Corelab and the Center for Impact Communications, where he advised Pakistani Nobel Peace Prize laureate Malala Yousafzai and Swedish environmental activist Greta Thunberg, among others, on their advocacy campaigns.

Populares crossed paths with Holmes à Court when he asked the communications group to evaluate Climate 200's performance in 2019 and give advice on how to improve it. They reviewed Climate 200's strategy, worked out what kind of seats should be targeted and gave advice on building a donor base.

Once the electorate-based community groups started forming, Populares was engaged by some of them to help with strategy from 'soup to nuts', Coper told me. It gave advice on how to run a candidate search and build a political campaign; then, when a campaign was up and running, the group's main role was advising on the content and delivery of the advertising. Populares was closely involved with the campaigns in Wentworth, Kooyong and Mackellar, and to a lesser extent in North Sydney, but it also gave advice to some of the other successful campaigns, Coper said.

Despite the media's tendency to lump the Teal seats together, Populares helped the candidates create individual campaigns that spoke to their differences. 'They don't look exactly like each other, they don't respond to the same messages in the same way, so it was not a one-size-fits-all approach. It was about treating each seat as a unique campaign with unique characteristics and doing the research to determine what those characteristics were.'

Coper did still recognise some common factors, including that 'all the candidates were professional women who had been quite accomplished and quite successful and that became an incredibly powerful constituency when the government was doing a terrible job of speaking to that constituency. And we saw this when they launched their attacks on the candidates; they really were applying a very old model of political campaigning that was designed for traditional Liberal/Labor contests'.

The sexist slurs that emerged from the Liberal side were completely counterproductive, he told me.

'Things like them being fake and having men behind them pulling their strings, having midlife crises to drive them to do this ... I think those are criticisms that every professional woman recognises in their day-to-day work life, the same sorts of criticisms that they would have to face in the workplace. And that really reinforced what drove a lot of people away from the Liberal Party in the first place, which was their treatment of women, their lack of understanding about the issues and the tone-deaf nature of their treatment of the issues.'

Climate change action was of course also a common focus, leading to the critique that the campaigns must be coordinated because they were all talking about the same topic. In fact, all of the voters in these seats really did care about climate change, Coper said.

The third commonality was the way they conducted the campaigns with integrity, Coper said, satisfying the voter's desire for a form of politics that was genuinely connected to the community and genuinely advocated for their values with no ulterior motive.

Coper was able to bring to the campaigns the benefits of his US experience, using cutting-edge commercial advertising knowledge and political advertising techniques, and applying them in a new way. 'So those sorts of things upended a lot of the orthodoxies of how political advertising is done in Australia and I think the results speak for themselves.'

The Teal campaigns spent a lot of money on digital advertising; part of that was by necessity – because starting from scratch with a smaller budget meant they had to be digital-first – and part of it was by design. Used correctly, according to Coper, digital advertising platforms are incredibly persuasive forms of advertising, while TV and newspaper advertising are incredibly ineffective forms of persuasion. 'You're not selling a pair of sneakers, and while those traditional forms of advertising have their place, using advertising for persuasion is a very different offering than when you are trying to sell something.'

The emphasis on digital, he told me, was also driven by the fact that the Teal campaigns started with a base primary vote and name recognition of zero. Any credible Liberal incumbent could get a primary vote of at least 25 per cent just from the value of the brand, but the community campaigns had to fight for every vote; to do that you needed a sophisticated advertising program, according to Coper.

He said that a few political shibboleths were challenged by the campaigns. The orthodoxy is that elections in Australia are usually decided by voters with little political engagement, who normally make their mind up at a very late stage. 'So typically, the orthodoxy says keep your advertising budget in reserve until the last six weeks of a campaign, but really escalate towards the last couple of weeks of the campaign.'

But now almost half of all voters has already voted by election day, so the election period has to be viewed as a whole, rather than just a day, according to Coper. The approach to advertising also has to take into account how persuasion works, he said.

'People think that they're a lot more rational than they are and that they will be presented with a suite of policies and then make their mind up on it when they are informed on the content. And it's not really how we form opinions – we form opinions these days largely by osmosis, largely through social media and the opinions of our peers and we don't really know we're doing it when we do it. So you have to view the persuasion window as happening over the course of months, not weeks.'

Very large-scale digital advertising campaigns were launched as soon as the Teal candidates were announced in each seat, designed to inform voters who the candidate was and what she stood for. These digital campaigns were supported with well-attended launch events 'to convey the groundswell of momentum around the candidate'.

Coper and his team calculated that the average voter in Kooyong saw an ad for Monique Ryan an average of 251 times in the months leading up to the election. 'A lot of times we would serve an ad to a voter in these seats and the voter would share it,' he told me. 'Sharing a Facebook ad is the best proof that it was a welcome positive message, because sharing with your peers is the deepest level of engagement you can have with it. And so what that suggests is that the advertising was particularly resonant.'

Anyone living in Kooyong saw two entirely different political advertising campaigns, the strategist said. While the Liberals saturated the electorate with paid outdoor advertising, such as billboards, Ryan's approach was to have her volunteers 'out there in the real world', walking the streets in Teal T-shirts, hanging signs on fences, and so on. 'And that was organic community advertising versus paid outdoor advertising and really told the story of the two campaigns, one not connected to the community and one connected to the community.'

One of the biggest miscalculations made by the Liberal Party was assuming that the model for a successful Teal candidate relied on the incumbent being very unpopular, like Tony Abbott in Warringah. They also likely miscalculated how popular some of their representatives were – including Josh Frydenberg. Kooyong voters, according to Coper, 'were given a very good reason to jump ship and never given a good reason to just stay on the Liberal ship, other than the remote possibility that Josh Frydenberg would be prime minister one day, which they didn't particularly welcome'.

All these campaigns raised far more money from the communities than they ever did from Climate 200, Coper said. 'The value was in the timing of Climate 200 and the security of being able to say that at least we have a certain amount of money secured from one donor, which in reality was 10,000 donors. Having that fundraising operation in place allowed the campaigns to be much more ambitious in their goals.'

One of the benefits of digital advertising is interactivity, Coper said. 'When you have ads in the field, they are generating literally millions of interactions with the people in those sites and you can tell very quickly if a message is working or not.'

For example, Populares believed Barnaby Joyce would be the most disliked Coalition figure among potential Teal voters. So, for Wentworth, the most persuasive message would be: 'Vote Dave Sharma, get Barnaby Joyce.' But instead of just trusting their instincts, Populares released ads that tested that message with other politicians: vote Dave Sharma, get Peter Dutton; vote Dave Sharma, get Scott Morrison. After thousands of people had reacted to it, they discovered that Scott Morrison was even more toxic than Barnaby Joyce.

'So the narrative platform for these campaigns became brand association with Scott Morrison, and, as you can see in hindsight, what became the main election narrative writ large was the country's personal dislike for Scott Morrison more so than the Liberal brand.'

Because of his US experience, Coper knew to overlook the so-called vanity metrics of an interaction with a digital ad (likes and shares), which are designed to track sales conversions. 'You need to be able to look at a Facebook ad and glean not how popular it was but how persuasive it is. And that's something that we've refined over the years in terms of our methodology so that we could tell persuasiveness, not just popularity.' The Populares team analysed interactions with a digital ad using its own internal algorithm that took into account dozens of various different data points to calculate its political persuasiveness.

The constant negative attacks on the Teal candidates, mostly from outlets owned by News Corp, were completely ineffective, Coper said. In fact, they were counterproductive because they gave valuable name recognition to the candidates, and reinforced what people already disliked about the Coalition. 'So putting John Howard on your front page calling these women "groupies" is really insulting to the voters in the seats … "More of that please, News Corp, that was incredibly helpful."' Accusations by conservative politicians and right-wing media pundits that the Teals were an ALP or Greens front were simply not believed by voters, he said.

Populares thought the Teal candidates would win their seats – even Mackellar, in Sydney, which looked a bit different. 'When you look at all of these seats, every single voter cares about climate change so it's not a particularly useful delineator. On paper the voters of Mackellar shouldn't be as likely to switch their vote as some of the other seats because they're significantly more conservative, not in terms of the political ideology or party affiliation, but in terms of their worldview.' Because they live surrounded by beautiful beaches and parks, they want to conserve that, in the literal meaning of a conservative, he told me. But the demographics meant 'the Liberal Party fell into this trap where they never saw Mackellar coming'.

RedBridge: Political nous
The other secret weapon in the Teal arsenal was The RedBridge Group's Kos Samaras.

The Victorian Labor Party veteran has a long history of crossing swords with Liberal MP Tim Smith, frequently jumping onto the political class's favourite boxing arena, Twitter, to lay into him. One night, Voices of Kooyong chair

Ann Capling was reading her Twitter feed and saw their latest stoush. Intrigued, she messaged Samaras; they talked and she arranged for him to speak to the group. Because of the lockdown, he addressed them via Zoom – Simon Holmes à Court was listening.

The two men could not be more different. Holmes à Court, the son of a billionaire and graduate of Geelong Grammar, had grown up a world away from Samaras' childhood home in Broadmeadows, a tough, working-class suburb of Melbourne. After leaving school, Samaras ran his own business for a few years before working as a political adviser and then becoming assistant state secretary of the Victorian Labor Party in 2005, after which he led several successful election campaigns.

After retiring from the Labor Party in 2019, he formed political consultancy firm The RedBridge Group with two partners. When he is not reading Stoic philosophy, the fifty-one-year-old long-distance runner lives and breathes progressive politics.

Part of Samaras' role in the Labor Party had been studying demographic changes in Melbourne communities and making predictions about the effect on voting habits. That night on Zoom, he described to the Voices of Kooyong how the electorate had changed over the past twenty years.

For his research, he had looked at the higher population density resulting from two decades' worth of apartment building and then asked himself, 'What is the social-cultural footprint of the people who are moving into these new abodes? And would that have an effect on the broader community they're moving into?'

'Because one thing we do know is that when people live in these tight-knit communities over time … they know each other, they hang out in local restaurants and bars and pubs and it becomes a community. And what happens over time is that the whole politics of that particular community changes with it.'

He convinced Voices of Kooyong that an effective campaign could lead to political change.

The next morning, Holmes à Court contacted Samaras and had a conversation that may have changed the course of Australian political history. The businessman said he'd been thinking about using a type of Political Action Committee (PAC), a US vehicle for raising and spending money on political contests without having a formal connection to the parties or the candidates. Most PACs represent business, labour or ideological interests and the largest ones, like ActBlue, raise and distribute more than a billion dollars each.

Samaras was interested, telling Holmes à Court that it wasn't just Kooyong. 'It's Goldstein, it's Wentworth – there's a range of electorates around the country, particularly in our two largest cities, that will be prone to a campaign of this nature.'

Helen Haines and Cathy McGowan had already shown that this was possible, Samaras said. 'We were entering the era of people wanting something different in their politics and we'd already seen that in regional Australia, where a lot of independents had started to get elected. And it was really only a matter of time before the people in our large cities started opting for something quite different.'

Samaras believed that these campaigns would be much harder to run in working-class communities, where people are simply trying to survive from week to week. They lack time, money and certain skill sets, he said.

Samaras showed Holmes à Court a list of vulnerable seats, but the businessman had already thought of most of them:

'I just simply provided the data to confirm that his educated assessment was indeed correct.'

Over time, Climate 200 and RedBridge started putting together a research program to monitor a select group of seats.

'First of all, we would be testing the appetite of those communities for a candidate like Zali Steggall. We tested it and we also did focus groups to see how big that appetite was in a qualitative sense. Talking to someone for an hour and a half is a far more beneficial exercise than trying to run surveys.

'And so we would say, "Zali Steggall represents the seat of Warringah. Are you aware of her? You know, she stands up for climate change." The answer in these electorates was 65 per cent yes. "Monique Ryan represents similar values, does this change your vote?" And we could see straightaway, early on, that it was going to change their vote.'

In October 2021, soon after she was announced as the candidate for Kooyong, Ryan polled 11 per cent; the next polls were 16 per cent, the low 20s and then the high 20s, Samaras said.

'You could see the progression. And so that gave us a really good longitudinal assessment from a data perspective as to how these campaigns were impacting the vote. And we could see that they were having great success in what they were doing; the data was simply putting a microscopic analysis on that community groundswell.'

When volunteers started door-knocking their neighbours to talk about issues, 'It showed people that this is a different form of politics. People living in seats like Goldstein, Kooyong and Wentworth suffer the same problem that people living in the community I grew up in do, and that is a sense of disempowerment from politics. That they are ignored, their concerns are not listened to and they have no power to do anything about it.

Well, in these particular communities, they've discovered how to do something about it.'

As so many former Liberal voters and even politicians were starting to say, they no longer recognised the Liberal Party.

'When it comes to the Teal seats, people voted Liberal because that was part of their identity, it's who they were, it's how they view the world around them. And the Liberal Party was turning a mirror back onto them and saying, "I think we're different from you." That's one cohort. Another cohort was the young professionals who had grown up in Liberal families but become more progressive after going to university.'

He points out that the vote in favour of same-sex marriage was highest in these electorates. This should have been seen as a warning sign by the Liberal Party, he told me, but instead 'they ignored it and just kept doubling down on this Trump BS; they wanted to move their brand of politics to something that was appealing to people living in the southern states of the US or parts of Queensland. That's not who you're dealing with in Wentworth, North Sydney, Mackellar'.

Samaras and his team identified renters as a group that could be crucial to victory. As housing prices escalate and young people continue to want to live in the inner city, the number of renters has been steadily rising.

'Like the industrial revolution, the housing crisis is creating a new voter,' Samaras tweeted in July. 'Over 5m Australians residents rent and 1.6m are experiencing rental stress [paying more than 30% of their income]. This new voter largely skews Left; they are indeed voting in their perceived economic interests. Education, work and income do not define them, their rental status does. Renters now control so many seats that a pathway to the Lodge is blocked without them – the LNP are paying a huge price for siding with asset owners.'

The RedBridge team worked out that electorates like Wentworth and Kooyong had high numbers of renters, more than half of whom were suffering rental stress. When young people who had been brought up in an area discovered that, despite going to university and getting a professional job, they couldn't afford to buy property locally, they became angry, Samaras explained. They blamed the Coalition government, which has traditionally been seen as the party of homeowners and landlords. When Morrison said during the campaign that 'the best way to support people renting a house is to help them buy a house', one housing policy expert described it as a 'let them eat cake' moment.[47] The post-election census has shown that the Coalition now only holds three of the top twenty seats by number of rental dwellings.

RedBridge polled the electorates once a month and then every two weeks closer to the election. Driven by the data, they started with a wide selection of seats and then narrowed their focus to the seats that fell on election night.

'Climate 200 and the local teams worked together to work out which seats were going to be winnable. And it took a bit of bravery on their part because the data didn't really show [clearly] until about four weeks before the election. So what we were telling them is: "You've got to have faith not just in the numbers but what you're doing and faith in the demographics. This is going to work; stick at it. We just need to hold down [the Liberal members'] primary below 40 [per cent] and we've won.'

A campaign veteran, Samara emphasised to Climate 200 and the campaigns the need to allocate all of the money to the winnable seats, a process he described as 'brute-force economics'.

The campaigns took about $10 million of micro-donations 'and then they smashed that into six seats. The Libs didn't know what hit 'em and no amount of money from the Liberal Party was gonna help them'.

Having well-resourced campaigns in these blue-ribbon Liberal seats affected the Liberal Party machine in two ways, Samaras said. Firstly, it diverted the money flow away from other marginal seats like Higgins, Bennelong and Reid – all of which fell to Labor.

'We knew that by pressuring them in these [Teal] seats they would overreact. Why did they spend $2 million in Wentworth or $1.5 or $2 million in Kooyong? And the reason is because this is their heart, this is where the political culture used to sit, this is where all their power is … By attacking the Liberal Party's very identity in these seats, it completely disrupted the entire Liberal campaign monetarily and culturally. When you challenge orthodoxy and you work out the way to do that is to strike at the very thing that this thing is born from, then it really messes with it.'

Early in the campaign, Samaras was confident that they would win at least two or three seats and that one of them was Wentworth. 'I was absolutely convinced; the data was just too good. [Spender] was already recording mid-30 [per cent] primary votes four weeks out and Sharma was barely in the 30s himself.'

* * *

In his book, *Facts and Other Lies: Welcome to the Disinformation Age*, Ed Coper explains how disinformation has fractured society, even threatening democracy itself.[48]

The strategist told me that, based on his US experience, he is very interested in defending Australian democracy against disinformation-based fringe political movements that might look at the Teal campaigns and try to replicate that on the other side of politics. 'We can't take these election results for granted and assume that Clive Palmer and others won't be successful next time just because they weren't successful this time. They can look at what happened, they can look at the US, so I'll be doing a lot of work in the next three years on strengthening the health of Australian democracy and our information ecosystem.'

And for Climate 200, what happens now?

All twenty-three campaigns that Climate 200 supported in 2022 were for genuine independents who agreed to prioritise climate action, political integrity and gender equality. Three in particular – Nicolette Boele in Sydney's Bradfield, Caz Heise in the NSW Mid North Coast seat of Cowper, and Alex Dyson in Wannon, a rural Victorian seat – came close to winning. With the right conditions, they could win in 2025.

Climate 200 has so far paid less attention to the Senate as it is a bigger challenge for independents. Outside the ACT, only registered parties (with a minimum of 1500 members) are situated above the line on the ballot paper, with individual candidates placed below the line. More than 90 per cent of votes are cast above the line as it is much quicker and easier. David Pocock succeeded partly because the ACT allows individual candidates to be placed above the line and because, as a former sporting hero, he had high name recognition.

Byron Fay said they saw the 2022 election result as a 'launch pad, not a landing zone'. While the group had done some polling in advance of the Victorian state election in November, no decisions had been made. However, Climate 200 had decided that they would be supporting the Teals and David Pocock at the next federal election. 'The community of donors were very happy to support the incumbents Zali [Steggall] and

Helen [Haines], Andrew [Wilkie] and Rebekha [Sharkie], although the contributions we made to their campaigns were relatively modest, because they all had the benefits of incumbency and were well established and looking pretty good,' he said.

And for future campaigns? Well, Fay says it's up to the donors, who had told him that the 2022 success had been their best 'return on investment ever'.

One major supporter of Allegra Spender, media executive David Haslingden, told me the whole process made him proud to be Australian. He spent twenty years working in the United States before coming back to Sydney to start a publishing and broadcasting group. He and his wife Alexa donated $50,000 to start Allegra's campaign and he also assisted with strategic advice.

'I'm very grateful to have had a good career and to have been able to say, okay, I might lose $50,000. [But] if you compare us to a small-town election in the United States – the fact that we could mount a logistically competitive campaign in a blue-ribbon seat in a federal election for Australia with that amount of money is an enormous tribute to our democracy.

'And that's something that I hope we all really appreciate and look after as we watch other democracies really struggle.'

5.

SIX CAMPAIGNS, SIX WEEKS

On 10 April, Scott Morrison named the date: the election would be held on Saturday, 21 May, and the campaign would last six weeks.

He told a media conference that the election was 'a choice between a government you know and a Labor opposition that you don't. Our government is not perfect – we've never claimed to be, but we are upfront and you may see some flaws but you can also see what we have achieved for Australia in incredibly difficult times'.[49]

Albanese promised to 'restore faith' in the political system. 'I can promise you this: I will lead with integrity and I will treat you with respect ... I won't go missing when the going gets tough. I will accept the responsibility that comes with high office. I will lead a government that repays and rewards your hard work.'[50]

For journalists, election campaigns can be quite boring to cover – politicians and their parties' teams are trying to stay rigidly 'on message' and avoid any vote-losing mistakes.

Because the conventional wisdom is that 'oppositions don't win elections; governments lose them', all parties are very risk-averse. This chapter does not include the big set pieces like the leaders' debates, the daily press conferences and picfacs (photo opportunities). Just because some of us suffered through them, that doesn't mean that you have to.

This chapter does cover the highs and lows of the campaigns in the Teals' seats. In six electorates, a bunch of well-meaning amateurs were doing everything for the first time; what could possibly go wrong?

Week one

The start of all election campaigns is always a shemozzle; it takes a few days for everyone to change gears and get onto a war footing. Most of the Teals started their campaigns in good shape; they had funds in the bank, huge cohorts of enthusiastic volunteers and high visibility. But in some of the seats, the polling was still not trending high enough to win on election day. Behind the scenes at Climate 200 there were a few worried faces.

On the first day of the campaign, Monday 11 April, three media sites – *The Sydney Morning Herald*, *The Age* and *The Australian Financial Review* – published stories saying that the 2022 election would be remembered for the record number of independent candidates. All were careful not to make any predictions about their success.

The Australian newspaper had its own unique take on the topic, quoting conservative Indigenous leader Warren Mundine saying that Holmes à Court was 'Clive Palmer but on the left … He's just one of those filthy-rich spoiled brats who think they … influence elections by spending millions and millions of dollars'.[51]

One event crowded out all other news. Albanese had a brain snap when he was asked the unemployment rate and the cash rate at a press conference in Tasmania. He tried to fudge it, got it wrong and then said he couldn't remember. It became the only topic of conversation for two days; various media outlets described this as the moment Albanese lost the election. On Wednesday, a foolhardy young reporter asked Greens leader Adam Bandt a 'gotcha' question and received an appropriate reply: 'Google it, mate'. Never has the word 'mate' been deployed to such devastating effect. Bandt's approval ratings shot up.

Morrison signalled he would have more to say during the election campaign about banning transgender women from playing women's sport. This was a gift to the Teals, who were all running in electorates whose voters had less interest in this topic than the cost of train tickets. Steggall said the PM 'should be focusing on issues that the vast majority of Australians are deeply concerned about, not engineering new ways to dog-whistle to the ultraconservatives'.[52]

Later in the week, Morrison delivered yet another fillip to the Teals' campaigns by effectively abandoning his promise to establish a federal anti-corruption watchdog. This issue was the second-highest priority in all the Teal electorates, after climate change. Labor said that if it won, it would legislate the new body by the end of the year.

Media speculation had it that the Morrison government was rolling out policies that would lose them the Teal seats but deliver them victory in the more conservative outer suburbs; the first part of that strategy was definitely working.

Week two

In an echo of what had happened with Blair Palese and the Wentworth campaign in April, *The Australian* newspaper now accused Goldstein campaign manager Sue Barrett of anti-Semitism. The campaign office received a large number of violent threats; Victoria Police gave advice on upgrading their security systems. 'We even had some of our volunteers in Zoe T-shirts being chased by some aggressive men who were threatening them,' she told me.[53]

A *Guardian* poll showed that voters in North Sydney ranked climate and the environment as a higher priority than the economy, and integrity in politics as more important than the cost of living. Good news for the Teals. According to *The Guardian:* 'With Scott Morrison placing the economy at the centre of his re-election pitch and playing down his broken promise to establish a commonwealth integrity commission, the poll highlights pressures the Coalition may face as it seeks to hold socially progressive seats.'[54]

A few days later, Allegra Spender's Instagram page almost crashed when word got out that former Ascham School principal Rowena Danziger had filmed an endorsement of her star pupil. The formidable Mrs Danziger (no one dares call her Rowena) ruled over Ascham, one of the country's most elite institutions, for thirty years. In Wentworth, her opinions count. She said, 'I'm also voting for Allegra because she is an independent. We need the independents to change the conversation and to change the agenda.'

The number of Wentworth volunteers reached 900. Unconnected to this, word got around that the volunteer roster included a relatively high number of men of a certain age and status. In a few minds, Connecteam – the app the campaign used to schedule volunteer shifts – had become a source of potential dates; a friend and I dubbed it 'Spender Tinder'.

Former ABC journalist Margot O'Neill was one of the volunteer organisers on the Wentworth campaign team. She told me her fellow volunteers were 'board directors, schoolteachers, medical specialists, business owners, accountants, consultants, lawyers and retirees from all walks of life'.

One day she asked a volunteer, Jane, 'What do you do when you're not folding T-shirts?' Jane replied, 'Project manager, engineering company.' Nick, a senior executive in a multinational tech company, offered to clean the office and was given the task of setting up the online campaign shop. Mother-of-two Eliana organised volunteer training and activity while holding down a full-time banking job and running a local wildlife rescue. 'Fred [Balboni], another volunteer who was a former international computer executive, coordinated the military-scale logistics necessary for supplying and rostering pre-poll and polling.'

The 'vollies' erected more than 4000 Allegra corflutes and organised more than fifty events each week, from handing out flyers at train stations and shopping centres to group coffees and walks, as well as town hall meetings and Politics in the Pub events. Two hundred people got up early one morning to wave placards at morning commuters, and around 700 people did shifts on polling day. The Teal Army was ubiquitous.

When a lightly coal-dusted Matt Canavan publicly declared 'net zero' dead, it was another gift to the Teals – it's like the ads wrote themselves.

In Sydney, former PM John Howard used the Liberal Party's campaign launch for Simon Kennedy, the candidate in Bennelong, to criticise the Teals. He was loudly condemned for being boorish and sexist. Labor candidate Jerome Laxale ended up winning the seat with an 8 per cent swing.

Frydenberg was forced to take down a five-year-old photo of himself with a group of boy scouts after one of them complained. Later, the chief executive of Guide Dogs Victoria stood down after she appeared (with a puppy) in an endorsement for him, which is strictly against the rules for a charitable organisation. With children and animals out of bounds, Amie Frydenberg had to step up and be photographed with her husband.

The treasurer's run of bad luck continued when Kooyong local and scion of a Liberal dynasty, Rob Baillieu, burst into print. His father, former Victorian premier Ted Baillieu, was a Frydenberg volunteer, while Rob was Monique Ryan's volunteer manager, which must have made family dinners interesting.

The twenty-four-year-old wrote in *The Age* that there was little difference between a moderate and a conservative Liberal 'if you vote the same way, protect the same selfish culture and promote the same lines'.[55] Good people don't attack their own state during a pandemic, or use charities and public institutions to advance their own political causes, he said, pointedly.

His words followed an opinion piece written by his father criticising the independents, saying that 'their targets ... are all high-profile, successful, middle-of-the-road, traditional Liberals – a tradition with which the independents feign affinity. But these campaigns appear other than they claim to be'.[56]

The young activist wrote in response that 'some people worry we are taking out the next generation of Liberal leaders. The inverse is true – they've taken themselves out of the next generation. If your vision of the future is a vision of the past, then you aren't the leader we need'.

In Curtin, the team putting up the corflutes around the electorate was called the Flute Force. One night, they were notified that an unidentified man in a white van was travelling around the electorate removing signs and putting them in the van. The Flute Force gave chase; when they cornered him, he shouted, 'Do you want a Labor government or not?'

At the end of the week, Sydney's *Daily Telegraph* had an 'exclusive' report saying that electing the Teals would end life as we know it. 'Eating insects instead of beef, vaccinating cows by drone to produce less methane and building office blocks from timber – this is Australia in 2030 if "teal independents" hold the balance of power after the federal election,' it said.

'Leading climate-focused crossbench candidates Zali Steggall and Monique Ryan want a 60 per cent cut to carbon emissions by the end of the decade in return for supporting a minority government.'[57]

Week three

By the third week of the campaign, the Liberal Party had clearly received some horror polling on Kooyong, leading to a tsunami of 'Save Josh' stories crashing onto the pages of the Murdoch press.

Holmes à Court was accused of being about to 'reap a bonanza for his commercial interests' in renewable energy. The businessman, no stranger to a Twitter war, turned to social media to refute it.

Frydenberg launched his campaign in Hawthorn, repeating the claim that Ryan was not 'a true independent' and saying the Climate 200–funded candidates were akin to 'a political party'. He told the crowd that Ryan's mother-in-law had told him that she was voting Liberal, which earned a great laugh. Not so much at the Ryan-Jordan household, which was unimpressed by Frydenberg taking advantage of an elderly family member to score a political point.

Ryan, meanwhile, spoke to media presenter Osher Günsberg on his podcast, *Better Than Yesterday*. She told him the skills she'd developed as a doctor were useful for political life. 'I see people when they're under extraordinary stress, because perhaps I've told them the worst news they've ever heard in their life. And so I've got the skills to understand people.'[58] She told Günsberg that to be a good doctor, you had to be a good listener. 'And that is something that I've brought to this role.'

As they had done in 2019, the Turnbulls decided to sit out this campaign in their New York apartment. This didn't stop Malcolm, however, from doing an interview on ABC Radio National on Australian foreign policy. When host Patricia Karvelas slipped in a question about Wentworth at the end of the interview, he said he was staying out of the election contest and that his only contribution would be to vote. 'They are both very good candidates; Dave Sharma is a very talented guy and Allegra Spender is an outstanding candidate.'

It was hardly a ringing endorsement of poor Dave, was it? I've heard Turnbull express more enthusiasm for crayfish.

The former PM did not campaign for Sharma at the 2018 by-election or the 2019 general election. As Turnbull wrote in his memoir, *A Bigger Picture*, he declined to write a letter of support for Sharma as 'the text they proposed was so disingenuous I concluded it was better I say nothing … I gave Dave some good campaigning advice, which he used to his advantage'.[59]

If it included the tip about banning Morrison from the electorate, Sharma took it, as the PM was nowhere to be seen – in any of the Teal seats.

In Mackellar, about a thousand young people attended a free concert and rally on 1 May in Avalon's Dunbar Park to support Sophie Scamps. Comedian Dan Ilic told the crowd: 'Integrity, climate action and empathy – these are things I'm looking for in a life partner, but alas I hear Sophie is taken. She will have my vote, but not my heart.'

Northern Beaches band Lime Cordiale were also on the line-up. Oli and Louis Leimbach from the group said it was the first time they'd supported an election candidate. 'We've never really got into politics before 'cause it's just so contradictory and a little bit icky,' Oli told a local newspaper. 'Now there's a big change of independents that are standing for things that we stand for, so it really feels like a moment of change.'[60]

In Kooyong, the Liberal team hired ten private security guards to find out who had been drawing swastikas and Hitler moustaches on Josh Frydenberg's smiling countenance. It's a time-honoured tradition for younger political team members on all sides to sneak around the streets at night, armed with a Sharpie and some scissors, usually after a few beers. Most campaigns allow for 'shrinkage' during the last few weeks and will come and replace your embellished/enhanced/missing corflute. Pilfering of Teal property stopped after Ryan said that she had inserted Apple AirTags into corflutes.

Former NSW premier Mike Baird said that the Coalition must learn from the rise of the independent movement across Australia and warned that no seat could be taken for granted. Speaking at the launch of incumbent Paul Fletcher's campaign in Sydney in the seat of Bradfield, Baird said MPs must reconnect with their local communities. 'Your number one responsibility is to connect locally, listen locally and deliver locally.'[61]

Bradfield has been held continuously by the Liberal Party since its creation in 1949. In 2022, although Fletcher retained his seat, Climate 200–supported independent candidate Nicolette Boele cut his winning margin by 13 per cent to just 4 per cent, bringing it within reach at the next election.

Week four
The Coalition's popularity took a battering in week four when Morrison told the Nine newspapers that a proposed national

integrity commission could lead to Australia becoming a 'public autocracy'. The PM stressed that such a commission should focus on identifying criminal behaviour rather than more subjective questions such as whether spending in marginal seats amounts to pork-barrelling.

This ignored the many survey findings showing that the public is not sanguine about government pre-election cash splashes in marginal seats or 'jobs for mates', regarding them as gross misuses of public money. A good example of the latter was the appointment of retired NSW politician John Barilaro to a New York trade role. The news broke after the election, but it became a huge public scandal and could affect the re-election chances of the NSW Coalition government.

The next day, former Liberal frontbencher Fred Chaney went into print to explain why he was an apostate. 'The party I joined in 1958 proudly proclaimed that one of the distinctions between it and the Labor Party was that the primary obligation of a member of parliament was to the electorate, and that to cross the floor, unlike the tightly caucused Labor Party, was permitted on conscience issues.

'My concerns today are about Australian democracy. They relate to the lack of accountability in the government; the blatant pork-barrelling, the use of public money for party electoral advantage rather than the public interest.'[62] The former minister went on to say that he deplored the daily focus on politicking rather than governing and the way the government was being reactive rather than active.

He explained that he would be voting for Kate Chaney, the independent candidate for Curtin, who also happened to be his niece. Another Liberal dynasty bites the dust.

Meanwhile, in Wentworth, Sharma's campaign could only be described as a total disaster. A post-election report to the

Liberal Party's election review said that 'inexperienced staff were trying to run the campaign without adequate guidance. There was no structure to the campaign and no roles or responsibilities allocated so that the real work of getting volunteers, doing street stalls and manning polling and pre-polling booths and logistics for election day were left to the last minute'.

The report, compiled from the responses of 104 of the Wentworth Federal Election Committee (FEC), comprising the party branch members, and submitted by FEC President Sally Betts, the mayor of Waverley, said that the Prime Minister's Office and Liberal HQ had 'completely failed to grasp what was happening in the Teal seats'.

'Information from Spender's campaign team has revealed high calibre professionals with experience in US elections, as well as local PR experts and logistics professions, coming together to plan a sophisticated campaign,' the report added.

This is all true, but Lyndell Droga and Maria Atkinson built that team from scratch in a few months, whereas the Liberal Party has been around since 1944 – where was its crack marginal-seat campaigning team? Sharma had a 1.3 per cent margin, so why was he left to scrabble around in the dark?

Because of the 'lack of appeal that the Morrison government had for young people' it was hard to get the Young Liberal branches to assist, the report said. Sharma himself had to step in and spend too much time organising the campaign instead of being on the ground.

This was in stark contrast to Wentworth's Teal army; the report noted that the Teal volunteers were coordinated on a 'professional messaging system'.

By week four of the campaign Spender had more than a thousand volunteers – by election day, the numbers would rise to 1200. Walking around in their teal-coloured T-shirts, they were her best advertisement, a form of social capital unmatched by the major parties.

The Liberal volunteers, mainly young and male, looked like members of the Young Liberals who were just putting in the hours on the bottom rung of the political escalator. I sometimes tested their local knowledge by asking directions to the best local coffee and was often met with a shoulder shrug: 'Not sure, I'm not from around here.'

The Teal volunteers, however, lived in the electorate and were motivated by altruism, not ambition. They held in-depth conversations with the voters while admiring babies, exchanging local news and even minding dogs while owners went inside the polling booth. The contrast could not have been more stark.

The post-election report concluded that Morrison was the single most negative issue for the Liberals in Wentworth. Liberal HQ had sent out material saying that a vote for Spender was a vote for Albanese as PM. 'This failed to appreciate that many voters were willing to vote Teal with the express purpose of removing Scott Morrison as Prime Minister.'

Week five

This was the week that pre-polling began. The booths were inundated; almost one-third of the total number of votes nationally – 5.54 million – were cast in the two-week period.

Zoe Daniel was so fed up about the ongoing unfounded slurs of anti-Semitism in her campaign that she instructed lawyers to send a letter to Tim Wilson. The letter – a concerns notice for the purposes of the *Defamation Act* – demanded Mr Wilson 'immediately cease and desist from making public comments, in any forum or medium, directly or implicitly suggesting that Ms Daniel is racist or anti-Semitic'.

Michael Bradley of Marque Lawyers said in the letter that in the course of campaigning, Wilson 'had been observed and heard to make frequent and repeated comments regarding "anti-Semitism" and "racism", unmistakeably directed at Zoe Daniel and her campaign'.

'It's extraordinary Zoe Daniel is trying to use the law to silence anyone criticising her policies, and also silencing candidates calling out racism,' Wilson said in response. 'I won't be intimidated by her campaign.'[63]

Support for the Teals came from a very surprising source when NSW premier Dominic Perrottet dismissed warnings from Scott Morrison that a minority government would inevitably result in chaos, insisting that democracy could be enhanced by crossbench MPs.

The NSW Coalition is in minority in the lower house and relies on the support of the crossbench. Negotiating with crossbench MPs was a useful process, Perrottet said. 'In some ways, it enhances the democratic process because when legislation comes through cabinet, you sit down with the crossbench and work through the issues.'[64]

I spent a few hours with Spender at the Waverley Park pre-poll booth one blustery Saturday afternoon, where she was swarmed with people wanting to talk. Two Italian men asked her about her mother's Italian heritage and they had a long, spirited conversation. Spender had to relinquish her Italian citizenship when she nominated to run and it must have been a wrench. Many women wanted to stop and talk about policies and family; people actually queued up to speak to her – I hadn't seen this sort of reaction to a political candidate since shadowing Maxine McKew in Bennelong in 2007.

One of the men, a Bondi lifeguard, cheerfully exhorted the voters to 'elect a woman to parliament!' It occurred to me that in all my years of covering elections, it was the first time I'd heard a man publicly support a female candidate that way. I went home thinking that Spender had a good chance of winning.

Polling booths were almost overwhelmed on the final pre-polling day as about a million people rushed to the ballot box. For the Wentworth volunteers, the hardest shifts were at Bondi Junction, where a cramped polling station was set up in the mall. Sharma's 1.3 per cent margin equated to just 1200 votes – the difference between victory and defeat – so every vote counted.

The Spender volunteers were trained to stay relentlessly positive, and say things like, 'Vote Allegra for more women in parliament.' Eventually they were given permission to say, 'A vote for Dave Sharma is a vote for Scott Morrison and Barnaby Joyce.'

Many volunteers reported that as men declared their opposition to Spender, their wives trailing behind winked at the volunteers while pointing to Spender's how-to-vote card, giving the thumbs up. 'Allegra's steely ability to remain polite and positive in the face of sometimes aggressive voters and hostile media like Sky News was extra motivation,' Margot O'Neill told me.

The former journalist described a morning on pre-poll duty as a determined older woman strode towards her. 'She pointed to Allegra's how-to-vote. "Her! I'm voting for her! More strong women everywhere!" and she marched off. And that morning, woman after woman, young and old, did the same. And I finally began to believe we could win.'

Polling rose so dramatically that by two weeks before the election, Climate 200 was fairly confident that all six Teals plus David Pocock would win. Word filtered out to the campaigns, where the mantra became 'No Fuck-Ups in the Final Week'.

Week six

Most of the Teals stayed close to home in the final week, staying out of the spotlight and trying to avoid any unforced errors that could derail their campaigns.

The headlines were full of speculation about how to vote in the event of testing positive to COVID, a serious possibility. The Australian Electoral Commission had enacted telephone voting laws to ensure that people could vote remotely, but the rules on eligibility involved registering well before election day.

Marque Lawyers partner Kiera Peacock decided to challenge the laws after being contacted by voters who were worried about missing the deadline and being disenfranchised. Her team estimated that up to 100,000 people could be affected. After they prepared everything to go to the Federal Court on the Friday to challenge the telephone voting rules, special minister of state Ben Morton announced at 1.30 pm that the AEC had extended the telephone voting provisions. A huge relief.

On Friday, a very desperate Morrison warned that voting him out would mean the sky would fall and Twitter would be running the country. He told a Brisbane morning radio show that a hung parliament would be unworkable. 'The last thing we need is a weak parliament where basically, you know, people are voting based on what Twitter's saying,' he said.[65]

Victory

The best place to be on election night is in front of a television, large drink in hand while you flick around the channels. For journalists, however, it is a different story. You spend the day going around various booths (in 2022, in driving rain) hoping desperately to find, in no particular order: a candidate, a friendly voter, an edible democracy sausage, a drinkable cup of coffee, a usable public toilet. And after the polls close, you head off to whichever suburban bowling club or RSL is hold-ing the party to spend the evening with several hundred of your drunkest, loudest acquaintances.

So at 7 pm on election night, we are back where this story started: at the Allegra Spender party at the Bondi Bowling Club. I found a seat in front of the main television and set-tled in for what we all thought would be a very long wait. But that was not the case – counting began after the polls closed at six o'clock and the first Teal seat to be called was Warringah, which the Nine Network gave to Zali Steggall at 7.40 pm. The room erupted with the whoops and cheers of the volun-teers, celebrating the victory of a fellow independent. Each subsequent Teal victory was an opportunity for the DJ to crank up the music over the sound of the crowds' jubilation, which was almost deafening.

The first victory for the current crop of Teals took another hour, with the Nine panel calling Mackellar for Sophie Scamps at 8.45 pm.

Just half an hour later, it was announced that Zoe Daniel had won Goldstein. In an ABC interview, outgoing Goldstein MP Tim Wilson alleged that he had been targeted by 'an unholy alliance [of] GetUp, Extinction Rebellion, the Labor Party [and] the Greens all abandoning their traditional stance to back a former ABC journalist'.[66]

Tink was next to claim victory and she promised to seek her community's support to 'change the climate in Canberra'. She promised to deliver 'faster action on climate change, an integrity commission, an economy that is forward-focused and action to address the systemic inequality that continues to plague our community'.[67]

As he reflected on the likely loss of several urban seats, North Sydney's Trent Zimmerman emphasised that the Liberal

Party must ensure it continues to represent 'the aspirations of the great urban areas that represent a large portion of the economic activity of our nation'.

'There is a driving desire in the communities I represent for greater action on climate change, for greater action in areas like ensuring there are genuinely more opportunities for women in our communities,' the outgoing Liberal MP said. 'We cannot ignore them, for if we do, winning government again will be impossible.'[68]

At 9.30 pm, Labor was declared the winner by the election panel on Nine TV.

Just fifteen minutes later, Zoe Daniel came on to thank her supporters, saying the achievement was 'extraordinary'.

She told the crowd that suffragette Vida Goldstein, after whom the seat is named, nominated in 1903 – the first election in which women could be candidates. 'She was so independent that she couldn't bring herself to run for either of the major parties,' Daniel said. 'Vida was not elected. This seat is in her name and today I take her rightful place.'

'But I have been so embraced by the volunteers who've worked on my campaign – that has been wonderfully positive. And I look forward to providing honest, sincere representation for the people.'[69]

In Wentworth, Allegra Spender came on stage at about 10.30 pm. She didn't claim victory as she felt the result wasn't conclusive. However, she said it had been a 'a victory for the community movement around the country. We stand for the future, not for the past. You've given up shouting at the television, the negativity and the spin. You've all invested in the democracy of the country'.[70]

Soon after, Monique Ryan addressed the crowd at the Auburn Hotel to say that she had not prepared a victory speech; she'd actually written a concession speech, which said, 'Whatever happens, we'll always have Kooyong 2022'.

'The government wasn't listening to us, so we changed the government,' she told an enormous crowd of screaming supporters.

An hour later, in Sydney, Scott Morrison came on stage at the Fullerton Hotel to concede defeat. No one remembers what he said – all eyes were on Jenny Morrison's blue dress, which Twitter quickly identified as a Carla Zampatti design called 'Celebration'. Was it a raised middle finger to the Spender campaign or a secret symbol of support? Jenny, as usual, remained silent.

Just after midnight, Albanese stepped up to the podium at the Canterbury-Hurlstone Park RSL Club in Sydney, looking a little teary. 'Tonight, the Australian people have voted for change. I am humbled by this victory and I'm honoured to be given the opportunity to serve as the 31st prime minister of Australia,' he told the crowd.[71]

Albanese became only the fourth leader to win government for Labor since the Second World War. He is also the first Australian prime minister to be divorced and also the first one to have a non–Anglo-Celtic surname (his father was Italian).

In his speech, the prime minister-elect pointed to his beginnings as the son of a single mother on a disability pension. 'Every parent wants more for the next generation than they had. My mother dreamt of a better life for me. And I hope that my journey in life inspires Australians to reach for the stars,' he said.

* * *

For the Teals, it was an historic victory, but not the most favourable outcome for them – that would have been a hung parliament in which they held the balance of power.

Over the next few weeks, they celebrated with their supporters, moved into their new electorate offices and started their new lives as federal members of parliament.

Five weeks after the election, reality hit. The new PM cut the staffing allocation for all crossbench MPs and senators to a quarter of what it had been in the previous parliament, leaving them with only one adviser each. Under the previous government, they each would have had two advisers and two assistant advisers, plus the electorate office staff each member can employ.

Eventually, the government adjusted the ruling, adding in extra staff for senators and MPs with large electorates. But it was a portent for the Teals: once Josh Burns won the Melbourne seat of Macnamara, giving Labor its seventy-sixth seat, the Teals' votes were no longer crucial. They'd have to find another way to prove their worth.

EPILOGUE

WHAT HAPPENS NEXT?

So on the first day of the new parliament, 26 July 2022, six community independent MPs collectively known as the Teals took their seats.

Their presence on the crossbench was a reminder to the major parties that the concept of a 'safe seat' no longer exists. If the Liberal Party can lose the seat of Curtin on a margin of 14 per cent, as well as a potential future Liberal leader in Kooyong, then everyone is vulnerable.

From the start of the campaign, the Teals consulted widely with their electorates and took their views into account. This highlighted the absurdity of party politics, in which MPs 'toe the party line' regardless of what their constituents want.

The Australian polity no longer has a choice between the unpalatable and the barely tolerable; voters don't have to search the ballot paper for the least-worst option. The Teals have given us a real choice, and it's only the beginning – straight after the federal campaign, groups started looking for candidates for the Victorian and NSW state elections. By the time you read this book, the Victorian election will have taken place and there may well be a new bunch of Teal state MPs. 'These poll results suggest that a similar dynamic is now playing out at the state level,' Climate 200's Byron Fay told me.

Members of North Sydney's Independent have begun holding meetings about next March's NSW state election and have identified the seats of Lane Cove, North Shore and Willoughby as potential targets. Denise Shrivell said that there was a mismatch between the views of the incumbent MPs and the local community. 'People in North Sydney have caught the democracy bug.'

In an existential sense, what does the rise of the Teals mean for the future of mainstream political parties? What could the federal parliament look like in three or four elections' time?

At this election, the Coalition suffered its worst result in seventy years, losing an unprecedented eighteen seats. According to journalist George Megalogenis, the Liberals (plus the Queensland LNP), which had previously held 34 of the country's 84 urban electorates, lost half of them.[72] There is only one Liberal MP in Adelaide and Perth, and none in Hobart, Canberra and Darwin.

But the Labor Party can't afford to look smug; it only picked up nine of them – two went to the Greens, and the historically Labor-held seat of Fowler went to independent Dai Le.

In fact, the two major parties recorded their lowest ever share of the vote in 2022: just under 70 per cent. If this trend continues, it may only be a few elections before minority or hung parliaments become the norm and our parliament starts to look more like Germany's – a patchwork of small parties and alliances.

The Coalition, in particular the Liberal Party, has been fundamentally reshaped by the latest ballot. At the time of the 2011 census, the Liberals held sixteen out of the top twenty seats by average household income, according to political scientist William Bowe.[73] But since the last election, the urban conservative has gone on the endangered list. The Coalition has ended up with just four inner-metropolitan seats (as defined by the AEC): the south-western Sydney seat of Banks, Bradfield in Sydney's upper North Shore, Scott Morrison's seat of Cook in the southern suburbs of Sydney and the Adelaide seat of Sturt formerly held by Christopher Pyne.

There's a strong correlation between education, income and living in the inner city; electorates like Wentworth and Kooyong are prime examples of this. Election analyst Ben Raue has been charting this group's voting patterns for a long time. Before the last election, the Coalition held fifteen of the most highly educated seats (more than 25 per cent of the voting population with a bachelor's degree or higher), a figure which fell to four after the ballot, he said. It also went from twenty-four of the richest electorates (median weekly income of $800 to $1249) to nine, and as above, lost twelve of their previous total of sixteen inner-metropolitan seats (well-established built-up suburbs in capital cities).

In contrast, the Coalition now holds all ten of the bottom-ranked seats by household income, which was not the case ten years ago.

The National Party or rural Liberals now hold the Coalition's nine safest seats. The safest urban seats are Cook at number 10 (31 kilometres from the Sydney CBD) and Alex Hawke's seat of Mitchell (number 16), which is a long way up in the north-west Bible Belt of Sydney. They are, culturally, a world away from inner-metropolitan suburbs like Paddington and Darling Point.

William Bowe said that there was a fundamental realignment going on in the politics of the two-party, centre-right and centre-left political systems of the English-speaking world. What was once a socio-economic class-based division is now harder to categorise.

Some observers call it the Nowheres versus the Somewheres, he told me. 'Namely the cosmopolitan globalised knowledge class versus the people who have a lower level of education, a stronger sense of patriotism and of place, of a kind of communal identity with their country and to a certain extent their race.'

At the moment, there's a war going on within the Liberal Party about whether or not they embrace this new division, the analyst said. Election post-mortems have focused on the deliberate attempt by Morrison to sacrifice the Teal electorates in order to try to win Labor's outer-suburban seats.

'They were really making a pitch for the high-vis-vest–wearing vote, the mining industry vote, which had once upon a time been a Labor vote, and they imagined that they weren't in trouble in the seats that they ended up losing,' he said.

Another factor in the Liberals' urban losses was Peter Dutton's anti-Chinese rhetoric. In November 2021 he pointed to China's military build-up. 'Dark clouds' were forming in the region and countries 'would be foolish to repeat the mistakes of the 1930s', he said.[74] Members of the Chinese community were incensed by these statements and turned against the Coalition government.

According to Bowe, the ten seats with the highest populations of Chinese-language speakers experienced a swing against the Liberals which was almost double the national average. The top five included three of the ten seats the Liberals lost to Labor (Chisholm, Bennelong and Reid), as well as Bradfield, where Liberal MP Paul Fletcher suffered a 15 per cent swing against him.

The Liberal losses at the last election have also led to a shift inside the Coalition. Because the National Party and the Queensland LNP now hold thirty-one of the fifty-eight seats, Queensland is the new centre of power, reflected in the election of party leaders Peter Dutton and David Littleproud. It's hard to see how these two men, based in outer-suburban Brisbane and rural Queensland respectively, will inspire voters in Kooyong and Wentworth to return their votes to the fold.

It's not just in the federal sphere that the Coalition vote has declined. Canberra-based psephologist Ian McAuley has been maintaining a table of the Coalition's fortunes in state and federal elections, from the Victorian state election in November 2014 to the present. He says that the 2022 federal election was the 'nineteenth of those elections in which the Coalition's primary vote has gone backwards'.[75] Around the country, there are only two conservative state governments, in NSW and Tasmania. The NSW Coalition government of Dominic Perrottet, currently in minority, is pursuing a progressive economic and social agenda in advance of an election in March 2023, while the Tasmanian Liberal government of Jeremy Rockliff governs with a one-seat majority.

These poor electoral showings have led to speculation about the future of the Liberal Party – has it reached an electoral tipping point? There's an intense debate inside the party about its future direction.

Someone with firm opinions on this is NSW Liberal senator Andrew Bragg, widely seen as a leader of the moderate faction – although he is quick to decry these 'internal labels'. The Liberal Party should not turn to the right, he told me. 'I don't think that the Liberal Party should become the Trump Party – it's not in the nation's interest for there to be that massive fragmentation. I mean, the two-party system has

EPILOGUE

been able to deliver decades of economic prosperity and social progress in Australia.'

He said that the Liberal Party was a fusion of liberals and conservatives on social issues. 'We all tend to agree on economic policy. I'm going to work very hard to ensure that the Liberal Party retains its broad-church status.'

For Bragg, a trained accountant, the numbers tell the story. 'If you look at the position of the Liberal Party now, your average primary vote in the so-called heartland seats (Warringah, North Sydney, Reid, Wentworth, Bennelong, Bradfield, Berowra and Mackellar) in the inner city [of Sydney] is 41 per cent.

'The average primary [Liberal] vote in the suburban Labor-held seats (Werriwa, Watson, Parramatta, McMahon, Kingsford Smith, Greenway, Fowler, Chifley, Blaxland and Barton) is only 23 per cent, meaning that these primary votes would need to double to 46 per cent to be in with a chance of winning,' he said.

Such a scenario is, he said, a 'pipedream' because the Liberal primary vote is simply too low. Instead, the Liberals should concentrate on lifting the primary vote in the eight heartland seats by 6 per cent because a primary vote of 47 per cent will usually be enough deliver a win.

But this doesn't mean giving up on the outer seats, he said. 'We should try and throw the biggest possible tent over the Australian people. The strength of our party is that we are a fusion of social conservatives and social liberals; we can appeal to all.'

In an article that Bragg wrote for the Menzies Institute after the election, he pointed out that the voters in western Sydney do not vote the same way as people in rural and regional Australia. 'There is no doubt that parts of Sydney's western suburbs are more socially conservative than the Northern suburbs or the east. The marriage survey showed that seats like Werriwa and Parramatta recorded a majority no vote [on marriage equality].

Some of the regional seats voted strongly in favour of marriage equality. On top of this, the last election demonstrated that many people in the Hunter region wanted a more ambitious emissions reduction plan. Attempting to tailor policies to all of these seats would not work, he argued. 'The cities and the bush won't agree.'[76]

The day after the election, Kate Chaney said that the result was an opportunity for the Liberal Party to have a good hard look at who and what it represents. Voters are seeing a shift in Australian politics, she said. As the Liberal Party has moved to the conservative right and the Labor Party has retreated to small ideas, it's left this gap in the middle.

'Communities are putting forward independents to occupy that space and it makes me feel very optimistic about the ability of our democracy to continue to change and develop.'[77]

So how will the Liberal Party solve these issues and ensure it survives?

Professor Frank Bongiorno has written several books on Australian politics. He said that when the modern Liberal Party was founded during the Second World War, the party's founder, Robert Menzies, deliberately avoided calling it a 'conservative party' because it was conceived to be a modern party that would incorporate both classically liberal and conservative philosophies. The founding Liberals certainly didn't want to be seen as reactionary, Bongiorno said. 'They want to be seen as liberal. And so it was deliberate, reaching out to a kind of an older tradition of liberalism that went back into the nineteenth century and was associated with people like Alfred Deakin.

'The cliché is broad church – it's a reflection of how the Liberal Party conceived of its identity in its early years, but then John Howard came along and changed that.'

The 1980s saw an emergent sectionalism between those known as wets (moderates) and those who were known as dries, and certainly the dries were in the ascendancy. 'It was a different sort of party that emerged in the 1990s, one that was much more wedded to a kind of anti-union position and was wedded to winding back of the state; it was very hostile to forms of public enterprises.'

John Howard has been called a 'conservative populist', Bongiorno said, describing him as a man who was more prepared to mobilise ideas around the nation and nationalism. 'I think there was a lot of that going on during the asylum-seeker debates in the early 2000s. It elevates national security issues and is perhaps less preoccupied with free markets than it is with mobilising resentments ... I just think we've seen that turbocharged in recent years.'

Although Malcolm Turnbull tried to move the party back towards the centre, he was unable to do it because he became prime minister in the midst of a kind of global right-wing revolt, Bongiorno said. 'It was in that election campaign in 2016 that Brexit happened, and then Trump, and that emboldened many right-wing populists in and around the Liberal Party and the National Party. I think that made his position very difficult indeed.'

Now the Liberal Party is in a position where it has embraced something that's really quite different from anything recognisable as a liberal tradition in Australian history, the professor said.

But it's not just the Liberal Party that is becoming less popular – the Labor vote is also trending down. In fact, the

Labor Party won the 2022 election with the lowest primary vote in electoral history.

This decline is part of a long-term trend. Canberra-based psephologist and engineer Ian McAuley has been analysing these voting patterns for decades; after the 2019 election, he created a graph showing that the combined primary vote for the two major parties has plummeted from 95 per cent, recorded just after the Second World War, to less than 70 per cent.[78] Since then, their share has declined even further. Labor's share of the primary vote at the last federal election dropped to 32.6 per cent (it was 50 per cent in 1946), while the Coalition's vote went from 44 per cent in 1946 to 35.7 per cent.

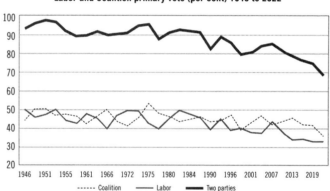

Labor and Coalition primary vote (per cent) 1946 to 2022

The flight of votes away from the major parties has led to a record twenty-seven seats, just over one in six, in which the final two candidate–preferred contest involved an independent or minor-party candidate.

One part of our economy that has decided to sidestep political games and forge its own way on climate change is the business sector. A Sydney-based fund-management executive (who asked not to be named) recently told me that a few years ago he had attended a business lunch with the cream of the Australian investment community, along with former Liberal leader John Hewson and former NSW Labor premier Bob Carr. The talk was all about climate change and Australia's failed attempts to meet its carbon emissions targets and transition to a post–fossil fuel world.

In truth, the 'conservative' parties were no longer conservative at all, the executive said. 'They had become parties of the radical populist right – trashing reason and science on climate change, thumbing their noses at market signals, undermining institutions, devaluing education, trying to revert to an imagined patriarchal past, and consumed by a cruel, irrational identity politics of exclusion.

'They no longer represented one of the most urbanised, multicultural, diverse and educated societies in the world. And now they pay the price for that neglect.'

Someone with a more than passing interest in the future of political parties is Malcolm Turnbull. He told me that although the two-party system may be in danger, it was more likely that it would be kept in place by our system of compulsory voting, ungerrymandered electorates and preferential voting.

However, the former PM said that 'it was a long road back for the Liberal Party because politics is very unpredictable. If Scott Morrison was a turn-off, which he clearly was, Dutton is worse. Matt Kean is the only thing that they've got going for them at the moment'.

In an interview after the election, Kean told Sky TV that the party should not move further to the right. 'The reason the party lost is because they are busy focusing [more] on these fringe issues and culture wars than substantive policy to move our country forward, to grow our economy and lift the living standards for every single person in the country.'[79]

Allegra Spender, Kylea Tink and Sophie Scamps should not have been running as independents, he said. 'They should have been running as Liberals because they represent our values and the aspirations of our communities. And the sooner we reach out to these people and include them in our party, the better off and stronger our party will be.'

Another moderate voice, former federal finance minister Simon Birmingham, identified more causes of the loss. 'You can go back to the same-sex marriage debate which dragged out unnecessarily long, but it should have been resolved by a simple conscience vote.

'I think the turning point was the failure in relation to the National Energy Guarantee. At that point, there was an opportunity for the Liberal Party to lock into a policy in relation to energy markets and climate reductions in the energy sector ... and the failure to be able to do so at that time has cost a significant price down the track.'[80]

In 2022, Professor Bongiorno wrote a piece for *Australian Book Review* in which he speculated that Australia's major political parties were 'broken, possibly beyond repair'.[81] He highlighted the irony of the major parties accusing community independent candidates of being, in essence, a political party.

A more justified accusation might be that in important ways the major parties themselves have ceased to be mass democratic parties, he said. 'Today, the parties conform to what political scientists call the "electoral-professional" model, machines operated by experts that are designed to facilitate candidate selection. This is a worldwide phenomenon, whereby mass parties of the traditional kind give way to organisations that consist largely of their parliamentary representatives and paid functionaries – a melting iceberg with a small tip and not much below the waterline.'

In addition, the major parties have failed 'to conform to even the basic standards that most Australians would associate with democratic governance,' he wrote. 'Factional warlords and party officers exercise overwhelming power.' An example of this was the recent controversy over NSW Liberal Party pre-selections, in which ordinary party members were sidelined and selections made by three people: the PM, the Premier and a former federal party president.

'Still, the independents, and especially those generated by the "Voices Of" movement that began with Cathy McGowan in the Victorian regional seat of Indi ... are offering a form of public leadership that, with some exceptions, has not flourished recently in the major parties. It is notable that their favourite causes – climate change, political integrity, gender equity – are among those that the major parties have managed most poorly. These are issues where there has often been a radical mismatch between public opinion and party action.'

* * *

So where does this leave the Teals, sitting in their new offices in Parliament House? How do they justify their positions?

All six of them came into the role with the extraordinarily high expectations of their electorates. But because the Labor government won a parliamentary majority and doesn't need their votes, they will have to demonstrate that they are more than just well-intentioned window dressing.

Independent ACT senator David Pocock is in a different category because the government does need one extra vote, on top of the support of the Greens, to get contested legislation through the Senate. Hence the presence of PM Albanese in the upper chamber for the former Wallaby's first speech.

As veteran political commentator Michelle Grattan has pointed out, lacking real power, the Teals have to operate through influence and advocacy.[82] Helen Haines' long-term lobbying for a federal integrity bill has linked her to the issue in the public mind, so the new community independents could follow her example and champion a particular issue. The issues they campaigned on, like tackling climate change and government corruption, are already Labor policy and due to be legislated.

Labor will try to stop the seats returning to the Liberals by giving the Teals just enough power – but not too much – to show their constituents that they are worth voting for a second time.

As fellow crossbenchers, they will naturally gravitate towards each other. But as Monique Ryan told the ABC's *Four Corners*, 'We are all alpha females. We all have to have a presence in Canberra and we will have to demonstrate to our community that we're delivering on the things that we've been elected to deliver.

'In many ways our priorities overlap, so we will each be struggling to demonstrate impact individually. And to a certain extent, it will work better if we work together. There will be tensions, I'm sure.'[83]

After the first sitting fortnight in parliament, Allegra Spender sent out a newsletter. In it, she said that 'it was an honour to vote for the first nationally legislated climate emissions reduction target. I was also able to strengthen this important first step with an amendment to ensure the government reports results for each sector of the economy including any subsidies or policies that might exacerbate climate change.

'Along with my independent crossbench colleagues, we carried the hopes of our communities into the Parliament, successfully proposing 9 amendments that enshrined greater government accountability for climate policies.'

A few days later, she told an audience of Wentworth supporters at a Politics in the Pub event that the independents had been able to have an initial discussion with the minister for climate change and energy, Chris Bowen, and then have a look at the draft bill, in order to formulate their proposed amendments.

She said that while Bowen seemed genuinely interested in collaborating with the crossbench, that will not always be the case. Also, there will be times when the crossbenchers will want to hold Labor to account on contentious legislation.

On the issue of political power, Spender told the audience that even though Haines did not get her own federal integrity commission bill up, she has set the agenda on that topic and been consulted by attorney-general Mark Dreyfus.

'And I think those are the things that you need to do, to actually help set agendas and [have] conversations about what is important.'

For a group of women who are used to having very rewarding careers at the helm of large organisations, it's hard to know if helping to set agendas will be enough to sustain their interest, long term. However, it is conceivable that if the Teals remain in parliament long enough the two-party system could turn into a multi-party one, with the potential for them to form coalition governments and become ministers. Allegra Spender as our Angela Merkel? Anything is possible.

ACKNOWLEDGEMENTS

With sincere thanks to *Crikey* editor Peter Fray, who suggested this book and has expertly overseen its writing.

I've been very lucky to work with the Hardie Grant Books team, including Elena Callcott, Kirstie Armiger-Grant, John Mapps and Emily Hart. Everything they have said and done has improved the book.

A large number of political experts generously shared their research with me; with thanks to Professor Frank Bongiorno, William Bowe, Ben Raue, Shaun Ratcliff, Ian McAuley and Margo Kingston. Former prime minister Malcolm Turnbull, Senator Andrew Bragg and other politicians gave me unique insights into party politics.

I learned so much from the experts at Climate 200 and their advisers, especially Jim Middleton, Byron Fay, Ed Coper and Kos Samaras.

I could not have written this book without the assistance of the Teals' campaign teams, notably Denise Shrivell, Sue Barrett, Tony Fairweather, Campbell Cooney and a cast of thousands in Wentworth.

In Wentworth, thank you particularly to Margot O'Neill, Fred Balboni, Jennifer Giles, Luise Elsing, Louise McElvogue and Nicole Abadee, and also Max Koslowski. Kath Naish who started Voices of Wentworth gave me important insights, as did Wentworth's Labor candidate Tim Murray who offered insights on Waverley Council, he is a tireless campaigner for his community.

I'm very grateful for the insights of David Haslingden and Jillian Broadbent and also the two founders of Wentworth Independents, Maria Atkinson and Lyndell Droga, who spoke to me at length.

To my family: Michael, Stella and Joe, I couldn't have written this book without your support.

Allegra and Monique – thank you for taking the time to tell me about how you really felt about campaigning and winning. To you and the rest of the Teals – Kylea, Sophie, Zoe and Kate – I'm looking forward to seeing what great things you all achieve.

NOTES

1   Brigid Delaney, 'Allegra Spender rides teal wave to usher in another independent's day for Wentworth', *The Guardian*, 22 May 2022, https://www.theguardian.com/australia-news/2022/may/22/allegra-spender-rides-teal-wave-to-usher-in-another-independents-day-for-wentworth.

2   Marian Wilkinson, *The Carbon Club: How a Network of Influential Climate Sceptics, Politicians and Business Leaders Fought to Control Australia's Climate Policy*, Sydney: Allen & Unwin, 2000.

3   Cathy McGowan, *Cathy Goes to Canberra: Doing Politics Differently*, Melbourne: Monash University Publishing, 2020.

4   Voices for Indi, 'Kitchen Table Conversations: Information for hosts', https://cathymcgowan.com.au/wp-content/uploads/2020/11.

5   'How the teals really won, with Simon Holmes à Court' (podcast episode), *7am*, 30 May 2022, https://7ampodcast.com.au/episodes/how-the-teals-really-won-with-simon-holmes-a-court.

6   Katina Curtis, 'Labor is red, Liberals are blue. What's in a colour? It's political hue', *Sydney Morning Herald*, 27 March 2022, https://www.smh.com.au/politics/federal/labor-is-red-liberals-are-blue-what-s-in-a-colour-it-s-political-hue-20220324-p5a7nh.html.

7   Peter Hartcher, 'How Morrison turns the blue heartland teal', *The Age*, 7 May 2022, https://www.theage.com.au/politics/federal/how-morrison-turns-the-blue-heartland-teal-20220505-p5aiyz.html.

8   Paul Karp, '"Doing nothing is not a solution": Matt Kean blames climate crisis for bushfires', *The Guardian*, 11 December 2019, https://www.theguardian.com/australia-news/2019/dec/11/doing-nothing-is-not-a-solution-nsw-environment-minister-blames-climate-crisis-for-bushfires?CMP=gu_com

9   Malcolm Turnbull, 'Address to the Smart Energy Summit 2019', https://www.malcolmturnbull.com.au/media/address-to-the-smart-energy-summit-2019.

10 Melissa Sweet, 'Why this doctor gave up general practice to run for election as an independent candidate', Croakey, 26 April 2022, https://www.croakey.org/why-this-doctor-gave-up-general-practice-to-run-for-election-as-an-independent-candidate/.

11 Voices of North Sydney, 'Andrea Wilson 11am session update', 27 February 2021, https://vimeo.com/517689853.

12 They Vote for You, 'How does your MP vote on the issues that matter to you?', https://theyvoteforyou.org.au/.

13 Margot Saville, 'Fossil fuel influence targeted in fight to control climate agenda in next parliament', Crikey, 23 November 2020, https://www.crikey.com.au/2020/11/23/climate-agenda-independents-election/.

14 Katharine Murphy, 'Scott Morrison's efforts to engage with women are more "me" than mea culpa', The Guardian, 27 March 2021, https://www.theguardian.com/australia-news/2021/mar/27/scott-morrisons-efforts-to-engage-with-women-are-more-me-than-mea-culpa.

15 Sarah Martin, 'Women abandon coalition, with fewer than one in three backing it, Essential poll shows', The Guardian, 29 April 2021, https://www.theguardian.com/australia-news/2021/apr/29/women-abandon-coalition-with-fewer-than-one-in-three-backing-it-essential-poll-shows.

16 Jade Gailberger, 'All eyes on Australia's debate over net zero emissions by 2050', news.com.au, 20 April 2021, https://www.news.com.au/technology/environment/climate-change/all-eyes-on-australias-debate-over-net-zero-emissions-by-2050/news-story/ba601f16b82a9bec3b899be8a3d21566.

17 John Daley, Gridlock: Removing Barriers to Policy Reform, Melbourne: Grattan Institute, July 2021.

18 Voices of Mackellar, Mackellar Matters Report, July 2021, https://www.voicesofmackellar.org.au/ktc-resources.

19 'Grassroots gloves come off', Northern Beaches Advocate, 3 September 2021, https://www.northernbeachesadvocate.com.au/2021/09/03/grassroots-gloves-come-off/.

20 'Grassroots gloves come off'

21 Jacqueline Maley, 'Meet the Liberal Party's latest problem: A climate-driven independent', Sydney Morning Herald, 18 September 2021, https://www.smh.com.au/politics/federal/meet-the-liberal-party-s-latest-problem-a-climate-driven-independent-20210917-p58sjz.html.

22 Climate Council, 'De-bunking Prime Minister Scott Morrison's COP26 speech', 2 November 2021, https://www.climatecouncil.org.au/de-bunking-prime-minister-scott-morrisons-cop26-speech/.

23 Margaret Simons, 'Independents and the balance of power', The Monthly, April 2022, page 29, https://www.themonthly.com.au/issue/2022/april/1648731600/margaret-simons/independents-and-balance-power#mtr.

24 Aaron Patrick, 'The short-seller and his wife going after Morrison', *Australian Financial Review*, 26 November 2021, https://www.afr.com/politics/federal/the-short-seller-and-his-wife-going-after-morrison-20211123-p59bgj.

25 Sophie Scamps, Launch speech, https://www.sophiescamps.com.au/launch_speech.

26 'Allegra Spender (independent candidate for Wentworth)' (podcast episode), *The Betoota Advocate Podcast*, 28 February 2022, https://omny.fm/shows/the-betoota-advocate-podcast/ep-200-allegra-spender-independent-candidate-for-w.

27 Michael Koziol, 'Unpopular Morrison to avoid Sydney's most marginal Liberal-held seat', *Sydney Morning Herald*, 27 March 2022, https://www.smh.com.au/politics/federal/unpopular-morrison-to-avoid-sydney-s-most-marginal-liberal-held-seat-20220325-p5a81k.html.

28 Koziol, 'Unpopular Morrison'.

29 Sharri Markson and Remy Varga, 'Anti-Israel advocate behind Spender tilt', *The Australian*, 5 April 2022.

30 Rhiannon Down, 'Spender "a lifelong friend of Israel"', *The Australian*, 8 May 2022, https://www.theaustralian.com.au/nation/a-lifelong-friend-of-israel-spender-denies-being-antisemitic-or-link-to-bds-movement/news-story/cd37edd964e0f56dd5a2d53c0849bd7e.

31 Royce Millar, '"Don't vote parochially": Who is Tim Wilson and what does the Member for Goldstein believe?', *The Age*, 16 May 2022, https://www.theage.com.au/politics/federal/don-t-vote-parochially-who-is-tim-wilson-and-what-does-the-member-for-goldstein-believe-20220515-p5algg.html.

32 Katharine Murphy, 'Former Liberal minister endorses ousting of MP Tim Wilson at next federal election', *The Guardian*, 3 August 2021, https://www.theguardian.com/australia-news/2021/aug/03/former-liberal-minister-endorses-ousting-of-mp-tim-wilson-at-next-federal-election?CMP=Share_AndroidApp_Other.

33 Sue Barrett, 'A message of support from Ian Macphee, AO, first elected member of Goldstein', Voices of Goldstein, https://web.archive.org/web/20220310121216/https://www.voicesofgoldstein.org.au/a_message_of_support_from_ian_macphee_first_elected_member_of_goldstein.

34 The story of how Curtin Independent was established is told in Tony Fairweather's series of articles on the NoFibs website. See Tony Fairweather, 'SERIES – Taking the WA Liberal Party's crown jewel', *NoFibs*, June 2022, https://nofibs.com.au/author/tony-fairweather/.

35 Andrew Burrell, 'Curtin candidate Celia Hammond spurns warming consensus', *The Australian*, 18 March 2019, https://www.theaustralian.com.au/national-affairs/climate/curtin-candidate-celia-hammond-spurns-climate-warming-consensus/news-story/30943c3e6a9e8c5cbed8f8bcbc79604f.

36 Paul Karp, 'Could a climate of change eject the Liberals from the Perth blue-ribbon seat of Curtin?', *The Guardian*, 15 April 2022, https://www.theguardian.com/australia-news/2022/apr/15/could-a-climate-of-change-eject-the-liberals-from-the-perth-blue-ribbon-seat-of-curtin.

37 Tony Fairweather, 'Taking the WA Liberal Party's crown jewel, #CurtainVotes – Part One: Launching Curtain Independent', *No Fibs*, 21 June 2022, https://nofibs.com.au/taking-the-wa-liberal-partys-crown-jewel-curtinvotes-part-one-launching-curtin-independent/.

38 Paul Sakkal, 'How a political novice took down Australia's treasurer', *The Age*, 28 May 2022, https://www.theage.com.au/politics/federal/how-a-political-novice-took-down-australia-s-treasurer-20220526-p5aoq7.html.

39 Stephen Brook, '"Like taking on Bambi": The children's doctor aiming to unseat the treasurer', *The Age*, 9 December 2021, https://www.theage.com.au/politics/victoria/like-taking-on-bambi-the-children-s-doctor-aiming-to-unseat-the-treasurer-20211208-p59fqa.html.

40 Melissa Fyfe, '"I ain't no Bambi": How a paediatrician ended up in politics', *The Age*, 23 July 2022, https://www.theage.com.au/national/i-ain-t-no-bambi-how-a-paediatrician-ended-up-in-politics-20220608-p5as9v.html?collection=p5b2e4.

41 Monique Ryan, 'SPEECH: Dr Monique Ryan reminds #KooyongVotes we do have a voice, we have a vote', *No Fibs*, 12 December 2021, speech transcript, https://nofibs.com.au/transcript-dr-monique-ryan-reminds-kooyongvotes-we-do-have-a-voice-we-have-a-vote/.

42 Margo Kingston, 'How independent Kate Chaney plans to win Curtin', *Saturday Paper*, 29 January 2022, https://www.thesaturdaypaper.com.au/news/politics/2022/01/29/how-independent-kate-chaney-plans-win-curtin/164337480013224#hrd.

43 Kate Chaney, 'SPEECH: "Beholden only to my electorate", Kate Chaney's pledge to launch her quest for #CurtainVotes, *No Fibs*, 6 February 2022, speech transcript, https://nofibs.com.au/speech-beholden-only-to-my-electorate-kate-chaneys-pledge-to-launch-her-quest-for-curtinvotes/.

44 Zoe Daniel, 'Zoe's campaign launch speech', 10 April 2022, https://www.zoedaniel.com.au/2022/04/11/zoes-campaign-launch-speech-video-transcript-10th-april-2022/.

45 Nadia Budihardjo, 'Independent candidate for Curtin Kate Chaney enters the federal election race as "the underdog"', Perth Now, 3 February 2022, https://www.perthnow.com.au/local-news/perthnow-western-suburbs/independent-candidate-for-curtin-kate-chaney-enters-the-federal-election-race-as-the-underdog-c-5482341

46 Margaret Simons, 'Independents and the balance of power', *The Monthly*, April 2022, https://www.themonthly.com.au/issue/2022/april/1648731600/margaret-simons/independents-and-balance-power.

47 Calla Wahlquist, 'Scott Morrison says best way to help renters is to "help them buy a house"', *The Guardian*, 30 March 2022, https://www.theguardian.com/australia-news/2022/mar/30/scott-morrison-says-best-way-to-help-renters-is-to-help-them-buy-a-house-federal-budget.

48 Ed Coper, *Facts and Other Lies: Welcome to the Disinformation Age*, Sydney: Allen & Unwin, 2022.

49 Sarah Martin, 'Australian election 2022: Scott Morrison warns voters against change as Anthony Albanese promises a "better future"', *The Guardian*, 10 April 2022, https://www.theguardian.com/australia-news/2022/apr/10/australian-election-2022-called-australian-prime-minister-scott-morrison-may-21.

50 Martin, 'Australian election 2022: Scott Morrison warns voters against change'.

51 Max Maddison, 'Climate 200 founder "Palmer of the left": Warren Mundine', *The Australian*, 10 April 2022.

52 Daniel Hurst and Paul Karp, 'Independents accuse Morrison of using trans sport ban as a "dog-whistle to the ultraconservatives"', *The Guardian*, 12 April 2022, https://www.theguardian.com/australia-news/2022/apr/12/independents-accuse-morrison-of-using-trans-sport-ban-as-a-dog-whistle-to-the-ultraconservatives.

53 Joe Kelly, 'Frydenberg rebukes Daniel campaign over Hitler tweet', *The Australian*, 8 April 2022, https://www.theaustralian.com.au/nation/politics/election-2022-frydenberg-rebukes-daniel-campaign-over-tweet-about-hitler/news-story/d2c17494c333ed4cc74f4066bce4e7d3.

54 Daniel Hurst, 'Voters in hotly contested Liberal-held seat rank climate and environment over economy, poll finds', *The Guardian*, 18 April 2022, https://www.theguardian.com/australia-news/2022/apr/18/voters-in-hotly-contested-liberal-held-seat-rank-climate-and-environment-over-economy-poll-finds.

55 Rob Baillieu, 'My father was Liberal premier, but I can't support his party', *The Age*, 22 April 2022, https://www.theage.com.au/politics/federal/my-father-was-liberal-premier-but-i-can-t-support-his-party-20220422-p5afh3.html'.

56 Ted Baillieu, 'Independents threaten to chop out next generation of Liberals', *The Age*, 21 April 2022, https://www.theage.com.au/politics/federal/independents-threaten-to-chop-out-this-next-generation-of-liberals-20220421-p5aezj.html.

57 John Rolfe, 'What Zali Steggall, Monique Ryan want if elected', *Daily Telegraph*, 20 April 2022, https://www.dailytelegraph.com.au/news/national/federal-election/climate-200s-teal-independents-zali-steggall-and-monique-ryan-hopes-if-they-are-voted-in/news-story/d66b1012f2 17b96543b574550bf6f091.

58 'Dr Monique Ryan and the revolution in independents' (podcast episode), *Better Than Yesterday*, 25 April 2022, https://play.acast.com/s/the-osher-gunsberg-podcast/429-dr-monique-ryan-and-the-revolution-in-independents.

59 Malcolm Turnbull, *A Bigger Picture*, Melbourne: Hardie Grant Publishing, 2020, p. 652.

60 Nadine Morton, 'Mackellar, independent Dr Sophie Scamps: Lime Cordiale, Angus and Julia Stone perform', *The Leader*, https://www.theleader.com.au/story/7720006/lime-cordiale-angus-and-julia-stone-playing-politics-at-rally/.

61 Tom Rabe, '"Don't take them for granted": Baird implores politicians to reflect on why voters back independents', *Sydney Morning Herald*, 1 May 2022, https://www.smh.com.au/national/nsw/don-t-take-them-for-granted-baird-implores-politicians-to-reflect-on-why-voters-back-independents-20220501-p5ahl7.html.

62 Fred Chaney, 'I was deputy leader of the Liberals. The party I served has lost its way', *Sydney Morning Herald*, 4 May 2022, https://www.smh.com.au/national/i-was-deputy-leader-of-the-liberals-the-party-i-served-has-lost-its-way-20220502-p5ahuz.html.

63 Rachel Baxendale, 'Independent calls in lawyers', *The Australian*, 17 May 2022, https://www.theaustralian.com.au/nation/politics/election-2022-independent-zoe-daniel-calls-in-lawyers/news-story/a28bb5f9c163a119b0575c120f0aa2ba.

64 Alexandra Smith, 'Minority government boosts democracy, Perrottet says, contradicting PM', *Sydney Morning Herald*, 9 May 2022, https://www.smh.com.au/national/minority-government-boosts-democracy-perrottet-says-contradicting-pm-20220508-p5ajir.html.

65 Catie McLeod, 'ScoMo claims hung parliament would be "governed by Twitter"', news.com.au, 20 May 2022, https://www.news.com.au/national/federal-election/scomo-claims-hung-parliament-would-be-governed-by-twitter/news-story/e7dd4657e4a750d731128933582057ab.

66 Daniel Hurst and Anne Davies, 'Teal independents punish Liberal moderates for inaction on climate crisis and integrity commission', *The Guardian*, 22 May 2022, https://www.theguardian.com/australia-news/2022/may/21/teal-independents-punish-liberal-moderates-for-inaction-on-climate-crisis-and-integrity-commission.

67 Hurst and Davies, 'Teal independents punish Liberal moderates'.

68 Hurst and Davies, 'Teal independents punish Liberal moderates'.

69 Hurst and Davies, 'Teal independents punish Liberal moderates'; Paul Karp, 'Tim Wilson admits defeat but other Liberal MPs yet to concede to teal independents', *The Guardian*, 22 May 2022, https://www.theguardian.com/australia-news/2022/may/22/liberal-mps-yet-to-concede-to-teal-independents-as-outcomes-hinge-on-postal-votes.

70 Delaney, 'Allegra Spender rides teal wave'.

71 ABC News, 'Read incoming prime minister Anthony Albanese's full speech after Labor wins federal election', 22 May 2022, https://www.abc.net.au/news/2022-05-22/anthony-albanese-acceptance-speech-full-transcript/101088736.

72 George Megalogenis, 'The future of the Liberal Party', *The Monthly*, July 2022, https://www.themonthly.com.au/issue/2022/july/george-megalogenis/future-liberal-party.

73 William Bowe, 'Census data reveals well-off seats no longer rusted-on for Liberals', *Crikey*, 29 June 2022, https://www.crikey.com.au/2022/06/29/top-end-of-town-takes-teal-turn/.

74 Daniel Hurst, '"Mistakes of the 1930s": Peter Dutton ramps up China rhetoric', *The Guardian*, 26 November 2021, https://www.theguardian.com/australia-news/2021/nov/26/mistakes-of-the-1930s-peter-dutton-ramps-up-china-rhetoric-as-keating-calls-him-a-dangerous-personality.

75 Ian McAuley, 'Weekly roundup Saturday 4 June', http://ianmcauley.com/saturdays/sat220604/week22060400.html.

76 Andrew Bragg, 'Pitch perfect', Menzies Institute, 8 June 2022, https://www.menziesrc.org/news-feed/pitch-perfect.

77 Peter de Kruijff, 'Chaney's change: Curtin expected to fall after independent challenge', *Sydney Morning Herald*, 22 May 2022, https://www.smh.com.au/politics/federal/curtin-candidate-kate-chaney-buoyed-by-eastern-states-independent-results-faces-nervous-wait-20220521-p5anbw.html.

78 Ian McAuley, 'Weekly roundup Saturday 28 May: The election', http://ianmcauley.com/saturdays/sat220528/week22052802.html.

79 'Kean takes aim at "distracted" Liberals over "fringe issues"' (video), *The Australian*, 23 May 2022, https://www.theaustralian.com.au/nation/politics/kean-takes-aim-at-distracted-liberals-over-fringe-issues/video/d0cde89778a4775e8e734a023172ca92.

80 'Simon Birmingham says National Energy Guarantee failure "the turning point" for Coalition', *The Guardian*, 22 May 2022, https://www.theguardian.com/australia-news/live/2022/may/22/australia-election-2022-live-anthony-albanese-scott-morrison-josh-frydenberg-teal-independents-greens-senate-peter-dutton.

81 Frank Bongiorno, 'Politics by other means', *Australian Book Review*, no. 442, May 2022, https://www.australianbookreview.com.au/977-may-2022-no-442/9088-politics-by-other-means-enlarging-our-diminished-sense-of-political-leadership-by-frank-bongiorno.

82 Michelle Grattan, 'Election delivered bonanza of crossbenchers but what impact will they make?', *The Conversation*, 30 June 2022, https://theconversation.com/grattan-on-friday-election-delivered-bonanza-of-crossbenchers-but-what-impact-will-they-make-186134.

83 ABC, 'Independents' Day' (video), *Four Corners*, 15 August 2022, https://www.abc.net.au/4corners/independents-day:-behind-the-scenes-with-the-new/14020206.